THE KEEPER OF DREAMS

Ronald Reng was based in London as a sports correspondent from 1996 until 2001. He has written about English football for, among others, the *Süddeutsche Zeitung* and Zurich's *Tagesanzeiger*. He currently lives in Barcelona, where he covers Spanish football for the *Süddeutsche Zeitung*.

THE KEEPER OF DREAMS

RONALD RENG

TRANSLATED BY SHAUN WHITESIDE

YELLOW JERSEY PRESS

LONDON

Published by Yellow Jersey Press 2004

2 4 6 8 10 9 7 5 3 1

First published in Great Britain in 2003 by
Yellow Jersey Press
Random House, 20 Vauxhall Bridge Road,
London SW1V 2SA

Random House Australia (Pty) Limited
20 Alfred Street, Milsons Point, Sydney,
New South Wales 2061, Australia

Random House New Zealand Limited
18 Poland Road, Glenfield,
Auckland 10, New Zealand

Random House (Pty) Limited
Endulini, 5A Jubilee Road, Parktown 2193, South Africa

The Random House Group Limited Reg. No. 954009
www.randomhouse.co.uk

A CIP catalogue record for this book
is available from the British Library

ISBN 0-224-06443-6

Tall as Trees © Ian McMillan
Writer, Broadcaster and
Barnsley FC Poet-in-Residence
www.ianmcmillan.co.uk
'You'll Never Walk Alone', words by Oscar Hammerstein II and
music by Richard Rodgers © Williamson Music International, USA.
Reproduced by permission of EMI Music Publishing Ltd, London WC2 0QY

Papers used by Random House are natural,
recyclable products made from wood grown in sustainable forests;
the manufacturing processes conform to the environmental
regulations of the country of origin

Typeset by Palimpsest Book Production Limited,
Polmont, Stirlingshire
Printed and bound in Great Britain by
Cox & Wyman Ltd, Reading, Berkshire

Author's Note

Before we sat down and started working on *Keeper of Dreams*, I told Lars Leese that he had to be absolutely open in our conversations, otherwise there would be no sense in doing the book. But I could have never expected such honesty and frankness and I can't thank him enough for it. This is his story and if anybody is offended by it – I hope not! – please just remember how brutally frank Lars is about his own mistakes and shortcomings.

Ronald Reng, Barcelona, June 2003

Note to Reader

The national league system in Germany is not exactly analogous with the English system, so here are the nearest equivalents in terms of level of skill and height of profile (details as at 2002/03).

- **Bundesliga** – the FA Barclaycard Premiership
- **Zweite** (Second) **Bundesliga** – the Nationwide Football League Division One
- **Regionalliga** – sometimes referred to in Germany as the Dritte (or Third) Liga, this regional semi-professional league was established in 1994 and is roughly at the same standard as the Nationwide Football League Divisions Two and Three combined
- **Oberliga** – a fully amateur league, comparable to the Nationwide Football Conference (with teams such as Stevenage Borough and Halifax Town)
- the **Landesliga** is next in Germany's pyramidal set-up, though it does not feature in this book; a rough equivalent would be the Unibond Northern Premier League, the Dr Martens Southern Premier League and the Ryman Football League, with teams such as Hednesford Town, Accrington Stanley and Canvey Island
- **Bezirksliga**, to which Lars' first team, Neitersen, gets promoted – a league such as Combined Counties (the likes of Farnham Town and Walton Casuals) would be closest
- **Kreisliga**, the lowest feeder league in Germany – Neitersen played in Kreisliga A, therefore comparable to clubs in the premier divisions of leagues at the lowest level of the English National League System such as the Midland Combination (Rugby Town, Southam United), the Northern Alliance (Spittal Rovers, Harraby Catholic Club) and the Herts Senior County League (Bushey Rangers, Wormley Rovers)

PROLOGUE:

WHAT DREAMS ARE MADE OF

IN BARNSLEY'S PACKED Oakwell stadium, 18,661 spectators were waiting for the game to get going again. They were waiting for Lars Leese to tie his bootlaces.

Sitting on the subs' bench, he'd started all over again for the fourth time: pulled the laces tight, made a knot, and tied the long ends all the way around the boot and under the sole, as professional footballers do for no discernible reason. Then another knot, and a bow. His trembling hands failed him once again. 'Hey! For God's sake, just take your time! They won't be able to play without you,' Danny Wilson, Barnsley's young manager, yelled at his substitute goalkeeper. He was trying to sound comforting. He sounded tense.

It happens in about one football match in a thousand: the goalkeeper is injured and the substitute keeper has to be brought on. Lars had fully expected the Premier League match on 26 August 1997 between Barnsley and Bolton Wanderers to be one of the other 999. Two hours before the start of play he had told his wife's grandmother, 'Gran, please, do give it a rest, I'm *not* going to play. I'm a substitute goalkeeper. Do you hear me? Sub-sti-tute!' Grandma Lina had come all the way from Germany on a visit to the redbrick family home on Winter Avenue in the Barnsley suburb of Royston, and she was about to see the first football match of her life – and she couldn't for the life of her understand why her granddaughter's husband wasn't playing. Before they set off for the stadium, she'd insisted on being allowed to take a picture of Lars. 'Before your first professional match,' she'd said.

'*Gran . . .*'

Two snapshots later, Lars had headed off with his colleague and neighbour, the Slovenian international Ales Krizan, and driven the ten minutes to Oakwell with a view to having a pleasant evening on the subs' bench. At first he hadn't even put his number 13 shirt on. He was sitting on the edge of the pitch in his sweatshirt, boots untied, when Bolton midfielder Jamie Pollock cannoned into Barnsley goalkeeper David Watson in an ill-considered tackle. For a moment there was silence as the spectators waited for Watson to get up. When the four paramedics carried him right past the subs' bench and into the stadium's catacombs, Lars wasn't looking. He was too preoccupied with himself.

I said to myself, 'A capacity stadium, and you're going to be a goalkeeper for a professional team – it's the moment you've been dreaming about your whole life. You should be pleased.' But of course I wasn't pleased. I had stage fright. Well, stage fright – I was bricking it. When Watson was on the floor my first thought was, 'Stop arsing around, please get back up again!' I tried to give myself orders: 'Don't lose it now, Lars.' And a moment later I was again thinking, 'Watson, please get up!' My thoughts raced around like that

during my warm-up. I pretended to do a couple of gymnastic exercises, but actually I couldn't stretch my leg muscles at all. My knees were so weak that I'd have keeled over. I swung my arms in a circle as I walked, trying to give the spectators the notion that I was really up for it. And then I couldn't even get my bootlaces tied. I felt everybody's eyes were on me. Eighteen thousand spectators are looking at you,' I thought, although of course that was nonsense, because loads of them were watching Watson being carried off, or just chatting to one another.

Watson had suffered a groin strain and concussion, doctors at Barnsley General Hospital would confirm the following day, but at Oakwell the cheerful mood returned in a matter of minutes. The spectators were determined not to let anything rob them of their exuberance. This was Barnsley's third home match of the 1997/98 season; they'd lost the first two, but there was still a holiday atmosphere at the ground. For the first time in 110 years the club was playing in the top flight of English football, in a league that is, along with the Spanish Primera Liga and the Italian Serie A, one of the most exciting in modern football. 'It's as though something has dropped on us from Mars,' said Michael Spinks, the club secretary.

The cheering swelled when Lars finally managed to get his laces tied, at the fifth go, and walked up beside the linesman, ready to join the game. 'Leece! Leece! Leece!' came the roar. After a good two months in Barnsley, Lars Leese – pronounced in German Layz-eh – knew what they meant and who they meant.

Before the six-foot-five-inch substitute keeper sprinted on to the grass in the 29th minute of play with the score at 1–1, Danny Wilson grabbed his arm and gave him one last piece of advice.

'Enjoy it,' Wilson said.

Lars wasn't so sure he could manage that.

I wanted to be like a tiger. Toni Schumacher, my childhood hero, once put it like this: 'The goalkeeper is the big cat, leaping at the ball as it would leap at its prey.' So I did my best tiger act – and nothing happened. Not a single ball came towards my goal. That's just awful for a goalkeeper. You can't be active; all you can do is wait. Your thoughts torment you. 'Let the first ball be a good one, and it'll all be fine.' And the bloody ball didn't come. You sketch out these horrific scenarios: the first ball a back-pass to you, but you miss your footing, kick it to your opponent and he sticks it in the net. That's the way your mind is going. It may have been five minutes, but to me it seemed like three quarters of an hour before the ball came to me for the first time. I dashed off my goal-line like a madman, out of the penalty area, out on to the left wing (from my point of view). It was a long pass into empty space. I slid over the grass to tackle the opposing striker, and there I was with the ball at my feet about two or three yards ahead of him. With all my strength I booted it high into the stand. After that, something inside me seemed to collapse and the applause and roar of the crowd swept over me like wildfire.

He can still hear the noise four years later in the living-room of his house in the town of Hürth, near Cologne.

Lars Leese is sitting on a blue couch, with a glass of water on the table in front of him, that evening at Oakwell playing out before his eyes. He is so stirred by the memory of that Bolton game that his pupils seem to gleam. This time he can enjoy it.

'It's all so far away now,' he says, then reconsiders his words. They sound wrong, because a moment ago, when he was telling the story of his debut in professional football, everything had felt so recent. And his time with Barnsley is actually a long way off in another sense. Lars is 32, a good age for a goalkeeper, but now, every morning, he leaves his house to 'flog pencils' in the Rhineland. That's how he refers, with cheerful self-irony, to his job selling office supplies. He's back where he started: Lars Leese, a friendly young businessman from Cologne.

His excursion into the world of professional football lasted only three years, but it will remain a unique career, because Lars Leese did what the rest of us can only dream of. Those of us who at the age of 43 slip on a shirt with the number 18 and the name KLINSMANN on the back, go for a kickaround in the park having made a point of drinking two pints fewer than usual the evening before. Or who, at the age of 32, smile at the supermarket cashier on a Saturday morning when in our mind's eye we're taking the ball off Andi Möller with a clean tackle. Or who, at 25, are playing in an ashpit in the lowest amateur league, dreaming that one day Franz Beckenbauer might run out of petrol around the corner, come to the sports ground and give us a job with Bayern Munich.

Lars Leese lived out our dream.

At the age of 22, he was playing for Neitersen in Kreisliga A, Westerwald–Sieg region;* six years later he secured Barnsley's

---

* For an explanation of the German league structure, see Note to Reader.

1–0 victory over four-times European Cup winners Liverpool in front of 41,000 spectators at Anfield Road. A part-time footballer had become a professional in the legendary Premier League, right up there with greats like Bert Trautmann and Eike Immel, the only German goalkeepers to have played in England before him. No one has ever risen like that before, and probably no one will do so again, now that the big clubs are sending their scouts off to youth tournaments as far away as Brazil, lest they miss out on any 15-year-old talent. But in this case a man who worked as a buyer of computer products for the company Raab-Karcher until he was 26, and who supported FC Cologne on the terraces on Saturdays, rose out of the crowd of spectators and found his way straight on to the pitch.

I'd been covering English football for the *Süddeutsche Zeitung* for two years when I first came across Lars Leese. My first thought on hearing his story was, 'That can't be true.' My second was, 'Hang on, I know this story.' For, just as unexpectedly, I myself had become a professional a thousand times – in my daydreams, when I went to the park in my Klinsmann shirt or tackled Andi Möller as I stood at the supermarket cash-desk. The truth is, of course most of us could never have carried off a career like that, even if Beckenbauer really had run out of petrol on the edge of our sports ground. Of course Lars Leese has more talent than the rest of us put together; he played in the youth eleven at FC Cologne before he gave up high-level sport at the age of 16 'because, like half a million others, I discovered beer and women'. But when we hear his story, with all the little chance events that helped to catapult him from the lowly Kreisliga into one of the best leagues in the world, we can go on quietly dreaming. What might have happened that time, in the 43rd minute of that school tournament

6

game when the coach of Offenbach Kickers was watching, if I'd shot instead of dribbled? What might have become of me if I hadn't pulled out of that regional selection team because I wanted to go to the ice-cream parlour with that dark-haired girl from Year 11.

During half-time in that Barnsley–Bolton Premier League match, Lars Leese still felt more like one of *us*, the daydreamers, than one of *them*, the hardened professionals. He spent only a minute in the dressing-room before Danny Wilson sent him out again, on his own, to face a few warm-up shots from the other subs. There had been no time for that before his hectic substitution.

It was just a warm-up, I know, who cares, but I thought, 'Oh, no. Just don't make any mistakes.' With some shots I didn't even dive, I just played the ball back with my foot: I was so worried the ball might slip under my body and the whole stadium would laugh. With every shot I caught I heard the crowd oohing in the terraces behind me. I turned around a few times and smiled at the spectators. I wanted to make a point of looking casual. Then the teams finally emerged from the dressing-rooms. In England, they always sprint out on to the field like madmen, looking like characters in a computer game. 'Concentrate, concentrate on the ball,' I said to myself like a mantra. Somehow I had to find my way back to reality, and fast.

Two minutes into the second half, the Macedonian forward Georgi Hristov put Barnsley in the lead, bringing the score to 2–1. From then on Bolton put pressure on Barnsley's goal. Daniela, Lars' wife, was in the grandstand.

Every time a Bolton player crossed the halfway line she murmured, 'Don't let them score, please, don't let them score,' and twisted her wedding ring around her finger. 'I thought I had to help him save the ball,' she said later. 'Somehow I wanted to beam strength over to Lars. I'd always believed that at some point during his training he would become better than the number one goalkeeper, and that he would get to play. And then it all happened so suddenly. I had no idea: am I supposed to be pleased now, or is it unfair to be pleased because the other goalkeeper has been seriously injured? My head was full of cotton wool. My nerves were in shreds.' At first, Grandma Lina hadn't even taken her seat next to Daniela. When she'd looked down from the main stand she'd felt dizzy. She'd clung on tightly to a steward, and although she'd only been able to talk to him in German he'd understood that she wanted to sit further up, under the roof. The steward found a seat for her. When Daniela turned around she saw that Grandma Lina was anything but troubled, in fact she was clearly quite content. Hadn't she said? Of course Lars would play.

Although Bolton were now dominating the game, they didn't create many chances. At one point a high pass came through the middle; Bolton's Peter Beardsley slipped behind Barnsley's defence and headed the ball at the near corner from 25 feet away. Lars automatically stuck out his foot and cleared the ball. On another occasion a free-kick flew over Barnsley's defence. Lars saved it.

In the press-box it was nearly time for match reports to be called in, and the journalists were having to come up with definitive judgements while the game was still being played. The *Sun*'s Michael Morgan wrote of the new goalkeeper, 'A convincing start for his career in British football.' Virtually no one in the stadium knew it was his very first game as a professional. Lars Leese had been announced in Britain as 'the man who had given up a glamorous future with Bayer Leverkusen in the Champions League for Barnsley', as Morgan wrote. In fact, Lars had been with Leverkusen for only a year as third-choice goalkeeper. Before he was transferred to Barnsley, he hadn't even sat on the subs' bench.

'Lars, stick the damn ball down the damn channel, for Christ's sake!' bellowed Danny Wilson.

The goal-kicks that had so tormented him in the horrific scenarios in his head during that first half went increasingly badly for Lars. He was supposed to send them out into the free space on the wing known as the channel, but Lars no longer cared about that. So long as he kicked the ball high and far and it didn't cross the touchline. So long as his internal horror movie didn't become a reality.

The final whistle caught him by surprise.

I had gone through the second half as though at high speed; the 45 minutes seemed more like ten, nothing more than that. You lose your sense of time, you're so tense. For 45 minutes you do nothing but watch the ball and anticipate where it could go. 'Where could my opponent play it now, how could things get dangerous?' Even if things don't get dangerous, all you see is the ball, and you tense yourself for what might happen if your team-mate misses it. And all of a sudden the game's over – a 2–1 win, the first home victory for Barnsley in the Premier League, a historic game. I don't know what got into me, I've never done it before or since, but my first reaction was this: I lifted my hands into the air as though holding an imaginary cup, looked up at my

**wife, saw her crying up in the stand and formed a
heart in the air. If I was a true romantic like Casanova,
I'd say that I did it because I could never have
managed it without her. The truth is, I don't know
why I did it. Not a single notion. In the dressing-
room the manager yelled, 'Fuckin' great, fuckin' quality!' He could have said anything; I was completely
reeling. I set off home with Daniela and her grandma,
and as we drove through the streets the fans immediately recognised me. Of course they did – we were
in an open-top Golf with German number plates.**

'That's exactly what happened, except for one thing –
you weren't there. You went home with Ales Krizan. There
was just Grandma and me in the Golf,' says Daniela, who
has put the children – Vivian, six, and Christopher, four –
to bed and has joined us in the living-room.

'So how come I can clearly remember what it was like
when the fans beeped their horns at the traffic lights?' Lars
asks.

'Because I told you about it,' says Daniela, and she tells
him again. 'The people went completely wild, they were so
happy, so carried away. They overtook us, wound down the
window and shouted "Leece! Leece! Leece!" I had to tell
Grandma Lina, "Stay calm now, Grandma, don't strip off and
dance on the bonnet!"'

'And I wasn't even there?' Lars asks, still amazed at the
tricks his memory has played on him.

Outside, Hürth can no longer be seen. Night has fallen.

**I didn't get to bed until about four or five in the
morning. I'd given an interview for the local radio
station Hallam FM at the stadium. 'Just ask me easy**

questions, I'm a bit over-excited,' I told the reporter. When I got home from Oakwell I just sat there and smoked one cigarette after another. I had a terrible headache from the tension during the match. Nonetheless I ran through each individual scene from the Bolton game in my head once again, even the radio interview. What could you have done better, and how? I reviewed the same moments – the corner, the free-kick, the guy from the radio – again and again until five o'clock in the morning. The next day I went straight to the supermarket and bought all the papers. I was . . . how shall I put it? What would you say? Happy? Yes, that's it, I was happy, incredibly happy, but happiness wasn't the strongest feeling. Funny, isn't it? No, I . . . I felt a mixture of a lot of pressure and a little responsibility. I . . .

He pauses, then starts over again.

I felt: this is where I get started.

1

THE EX-INTERNATIONAL

O N THE DRIVE into the Westerwald, Lars Leese smoked three cigarettes: one on the A3 as far as Hennef, one on the B road towards Altenkirchen, one to the junction for Neitersen. He thought it would help him win the match he was about to play. Not the smoking itself, but the fact that the three Marlboros followed the rhythm of motorway, B road, town. He was superstitious about things like that. Later, on the many Sundays that followed, he would stick religiously to that ritual. It was on 3 September 1989, on the way from Cologne to his first game for Sportfreunde Neitersen, that he first started it.

He had bigger matches behind him, games in which he had been playing for nothing less than his future in professional football – or at least that was that he had believed back then, when he played as goalkeeper in the under-16 side of three-times German champions FC Cologne. Three years had passed since then. Now he would be in goal again for the first time in a championship match, in Kreisliga A, just a couple of steps up from Kreisliga C, the lowest division in Germany. Amateur sport.

If people who have never played in a local league, or who would never think of doing so, went along one Sunday to see a game played by 22 more or (mostly) less athletic men on a sticky ashpit, they might think it's just a bit of harmless fun. That couldn't be further from the truth. It's serious stuff. Kreisliga players buy football boots for 249 marks (£79.99) and imagine they'll help them to put in better crosses; after all, they are the boots David Beckham wears. Kreisliga teams made up entirely of architects, office buyers and roofers go running in the woods three times a week in July, but not for the rest of the year. They don't need to, they've already got themselves fit for the season.

When I went to Neitersen 12 years later, on Lars Leese's trail, I felt I was grown up enough not to take the keenness of the Kreisliga players too seriously. And then, one cool summer afternoon, I sat with Jürgen Sanner, one of Lars' former team-mates, at the sports ground in Neitersen, and as we talked about Lars we were gripped with enthusiasm. We looked at that pitiful, abandoned ashpit and started to talk about our modest, unimportant victories in amateur football. 'When we became Kreisliga champions in 1991, I stopped. I felt things couldn't get any better for me,' Sanner said, and it sounded as though he was confiding an intimate secret to me. And of course I understood him: only Kreisliga players know that their sporting lives are probably not going to get much better than a local derby victory over a team like Eintracht Guckheim. But that doesn't stop them from believing in the importance of their game.

Lars, who could tell the difference between FC Cologne and Sportfreunde Neitersen, between ambitious and amateurish football, should have smiled at the determination of the weekend players. But he was the worst of the lot. When he turned up for his first game in the Westerwald that Sunday he had to go to the toilet three times. And that had nothing to do with superstition.

There's just as much pressure in a Kreisliga game as there is in a Bundesliga match. I said that in Neitersen, and I really believed it. Because I put myself under so much pressure, because I concentrated on the match for so long beforehand that I couldn't imagine anyone being under any more pressure than that. It never even occurred to me that the amount of pressure might have something to do with whether you are being watched by 18,000 or 180 spectators. You don't often get 18,000 spectators in the Kreisliga.

Word had already spread about Lars Leese throughout the Westerwald. 'EX-INTERNATIONAL KEEPER LARS LESER IN NEITERSEN' the *Rhein-Zeitung* proclaimed; Sportfreunde Neitersen had taken on a 20-year-old former youth international goalkeeper from Cologne and would be using him for the first time on Sunday in their away game against SV Alsdorf. The headline was a bit bigger than the one next to it, about the women's handball team from Weyerbusch, but the tone of the report was just as sober, just as unexcited. As though a former youth international turned up in the Westerwald every few weeks to play in an amateur division near the bottom of Germany's league structure. The article managed to get a few minor details slightly wrong – other than Lars' surname. The name of the youth selection team for which he had played at the age of 14 had actually been Mittelrhein, not Germany. But no one on that Sunday at the sports ground in Alsdorf was particularly troubled.

Normally about 100 to 150 spectators would have been standing on the sidelines, near the beer stall; at the Neitersen match there were only 40. The remaining 80 or 90 had formed a mob behind Lars' goal.

Not long after kick-off, Alsdorf got a corner and Lars heard one of their players shouting, 'Come on, get one past the international!' But that didn't happen that afternoon. Even if he didn't quite play like an international, Lars did enough not to do his new reputation any harm. On Monday, the *Rhein-Zeitung* rewarded his performance with an article of a length usually reserved for a Kreisliga game. The report on the match comprised a single sentence: 'In Alsdorf, the game between coach Roland Kölsch's protégés and Sportfreunde Nietersen ended in a goalless draw in line with the performances.'

That stuff about the youth international goalkeeper may not have been quite correct, but in essence, says Rudolf Bellersheim, chairman and enthusiastic patron of Sportfreunde Neitersen, it was true. 'Lars was better than goalkeepers in the Westerwald usually are,' he claims over lunch in his house in Neitersen.

'He saved every penalty!' Bellersheim's son Arnd butts in enthusiastically.

'Yeah. You see the legends that are still circulating about Lars hereabouts, even 12 years later,' says Bellersheim senior.

On the road out of the village, his name is written in letters as big as those on the sign for the next village. WALTER-SCHEN 3 KM it says on the yellow signpost, BELLERSHEIM on the white one above it. It refers to his petrol company, which he runs with his brother Horst. With 20 filling stations and 180 employees, Bellersheim rules over the community the way big businessmen in small villages often do, personal and patriarchal at the same time. Most people in the village call him 'Bello', and he thinks nothing of sending one of his employees into the forest at lunchtime to take Carlo, his young dog, to do his business.

'He's bound to tell you the story about Schalke,' Leese had said to me, and sure enough, Rudolf Bellersheim, 56 years old, eyes gleaming, tells of how, once in his life, he played a friendly against the great Schalke 04 (seven times Bundisliga champions) for Altenkirchen, a nearby village team. 'Football,' says Bellersheim with a sigh. Sometimes, he says, he doesn't go to the sports ground in Neitersen to watch because he thinks to himself, 'You can't go and stand at the sports ground every Sunday.' But then he can hardly bear to hear the results of a team in which he invests a little of his fortune from one year to the next. And he only phones a quarter of an hour after the end of a match. To do so any earlier would bring bad luck.

'But, now, let me have a think,' he continues. 'We're always saying "Lars introduced that" – but what?'

He thinks out loud.

'The long throw. Of course!'

He mumbles to himself.

'And shouting *Leo!*'

But surely that's an old story: when the goalkeeper shouts the code word Leo, the defenders know to keep their heads down, and the keeper comes out to claim the ball. That's been done on German football grounds for decades; Lars Leese can't possibly have introduced it.

'Well, OK,' says Bellersheim, 'but he was the first one to do it properly. *Leooo!* Really loud, you know, and *bang!*, he's taken the cross. He had complete control of the penalty area.'

But there was something else as well, for Bellersheim goes on thinking.

'That's it! When we were lagging behind and we got a corner shortly before the end, there was Lars right up at the front, trying to head in a goal. The goalkeeper, in the opponents' penalty area! No one in the Westerwald had ever seen anything like it.'

So the rumour quickly spread that they had a high-flier in Neitersen. But the mystery remained: why had this goalkeeper ended up there, of all places? Why did a 20-year-old from Cologne borrow his mother's VW Golf every week and drive 69 kilometres there and 69 kilometres back to play in a league for which he was clearly overqualified? To play in a village with 850 inhabitants he had never heard of before? There were plenty of theories. Footballers like nothing more than a good rumour, and in this respect at least Kreisliga weekend players are no different from the professionals. On Monday morning at the workplace, the news about the Sunday games is passed on, and on Tuesday evening after training in the dressing-room of dozens of village clubs impressions are formed and fixed. And when Friday evening arrives in rural areas such as the Westerwald, where the villages have quaint names like Oberirsen and Mittelirsen but the bars are called Cheyenne or Gecko, by the seventh beer rumours have turned into myths.

They've got a job for Leese in Neitersen. This fantastic job. And at lunchtime he goes training.

But, as quickly as it had formed, the idea was revealed to be false. During his first year of playing in Neitersen, Lars was finishing his technical exams at business school, and he later trained as a wholesale and foreign sales rep with Rover in Cologne. Still, the rumour persisted.

Leese is coining it down in Neitersen. He's making more than a Zweite Bundesliga player. And it's all tax free.

It's a favourite topic of conversation in amateur football – the huge sums of money some players earn from their kickabouts. Even down in the lowest divisions there are some players who get 1,500 marks (about £500) a month, cash in hand, from the local electrical goods trader or car dealer for two lots of training and one game a week. Every amateur footballer who takes himself at all seriously knows such a player, or at least claims to have heard of one from a friend of a friend. In the end, many Kreisliga players come to believe that such payments are the norm – but only at other clubs, of course. In fact, most of them play for the 10 marks (£3.50) bonus if they win and a free dinner in the club canteen. But who's interested in the truth of the matter when it's so boring? Thanks to the commitment of Herr Bellersheim the businessman, Sportfreunde Neitersen were prime candidates for the wilder realms of speculation.

'"Here comes FC Bellersheim," they always say,' Bellersheim remarks, and it's hard to tell if he's hurt or proud. 'Bayern Munich get big-time envy: we have it small-time.'

In his first season, 1989/90, Lars really did get 300 marks (£100) a month in expenses, most of it spent on petrol, plus 30 marks (£10) as a victory bonus. In the summer of 1990, when he was wondering out loud whether it really was worth all that driving, Bellersheim dispelled any doubts the goalkeeper harboured before the start of the season by giving him an extra 3,000 marks (£1,000). Expense allowance, they call it in the Kreisliga. But Lars could have got that kind of money in Cologne from another amateur club, so again, why travel to Neitersen? There was only one possible explanation.

He's gay!
He can't show his face in Cologne!
Leese is a poof!

It seemed that explained everything. To almost every game, and often even to training, Lars brought his best friend Holger Wacker along. They had been classmates at school. Three years earlier, aged seventeen, they'd even been held back a year together. So, not only did it seem perverse to some people in the Westerwald that someone from Cologne should come to Kreisliga games in Neitersen, he also always had a man with him who didn't even play football himself.

Leese is a poof, Leese is a poof!

But it turned out quite quickly that that theory didn't stand up either, because Lars didn't just impress his team-mates with his casual manner; on Fridays at the disco he swept the girls off their feet as well. His friend Holger came along because he liked it in the provinces, and he liked the girls, the companionship, the popularity enjoyed by his close friend Lars.

Still, if he only got pocket money out of it and he wasn't a poof, why did Lars Leese go to Neitersen to play football?

When I told my friends in Cologne, 'Guys, I'm play-ing in the Westerwald from now on,' they answered, 'Are you round the bend or what? Driving all that distance just to play in the Kreisliga? You could do that in Cologne on any street-corner.' So I just lied to them, and told them I was getting loads of money in Neitersen. Then they said, 'Oh, fine. We'd do the same.' I couldn't tell them the truth; I didn't even know myself why I went all the way there once or twice a week to train and play. It had started when I happened to be playing in a pub-side tournament in the Westerwald and someone from Neitersen showed up: hey, I was really fantastic; did I fancy playing for them at some point in the future? Maybe

that was it: I felt that there was still someone, some-where, even if they were in the back of beyond, who thought highly of me as a footballer. They gave me that feeling in Neitersen. It didn't matter that it was at the lowest level, all of a sudden I was seen as a great keeper. Maybe that was it. Maybe I had always craved that recognition since I'd first chucked the ball away in an attack of adolescent rage when I was playing for FC Cologne – but actually it goes back further than that, to when I was 13, in fact.

Very few children who play for a professional club at the age of 13 think they're in with a good chance of one day being professional footballers; most children who play for a professional club at the age of 13 *know* that they will one day be professional footballers. The idea that they mightn't make it is absolutely unthinkable. The fact that there are thousands of boys with the same dream, but only about 950 professional jobs in Germany, doesn't occur to them. Not at 13. It's an age when children are wooed from a radius of up to 100 kilometres by Bundesliga teams. Lars Leese was selected by FC, as the city's first club is known in Cologne, as though there is only one FC in the whole world. Until then Lars had played for SC Fortuna – the second, smaller professional club in the city – and in Klettenberg Park practically every day before and after school until nightfall.

At least there he wasn't alone. He was seven when his parents divorced. All of a sudden the flat in Luxemburger Strasse was empty. Ute Leese had moved out to live with her new husband in Hürth, and Lars' sister Tamara went with her; Wolfgang Leese, who kept custody of Lars, was at work, in a railway signal box. Even today, Lars Leese can't bear to come home to an empty flat.

He made the park his home. On the way there, down Luxemburger Strasse, a long, wide arterial road to the south of Cologne, he passed a driving school. He often spat against the window. He thought a monster lived behind it.

My father had dinned that into me. The driving school belonged to my stepfather, and he was the monster who had stolen my mother. When you're seven you tend to believe what your father says, and my father was my hero. Sometimes he took me to his workplace, and we would spend hours kicking a ball about in his signal box; it made far more of a racket than any railway train. He was the striker and I was the goalkeeper, of course. He couldn't get over the fact that my mother had left him, and for a friend of the family. I was just to have nothing more to do with them – he was forever telling me that. He would even stand at the window with a stopwatch when I went to school in the morning, because my mother still ran her stationery shop right beside our flat in Luxemburger Strasse. My father used the stopwatch to check how quickly I got to the next corner, that I didn't go into my mother's shop. But there was an awning above my mother's shop so my father couldn't see that my mother was standing by the door to give me a quick kiss and a bun for breaktime.

When Lars was 11, his father went into hospital with pancreas problems. Wolfgang didn't want to leave his son with his mother even for such a short time, so Lars lodged with a friend from the Fortuna youth team in the south Cologne working-class district of Zollstock. The flat there was anything but empty, but among the family's four children he felt more alone than ever. One of the children was always screaming, and then their mother would start screaming too. He was appalled by the woman, and watched more in horror than astonishment as she opened tins with her teeth in the kitchen. After a fortnight he ran weeping into his mother's stationery shop.

'What have I got a mother for?' Lars asked.

'You can stay with us,' said Ute.

That evening he came face to face with his stepfather for the first time. Nervously, Lars wondered, 'Am I allowed to talk to him now, or do I have to confess to my father that I've been in the monster's house?'

Meanwhile, in the hospital, Wolfgang met a new woman and didn't put up a great deal of resistance when his wife asked for custody of her son.

By the time FC Cologne knocked on his door, Lars Leese had already spent two years living with his mother and step-father on the Hahnenstrasse estate in the suburb of Hürth. He no longer played football in Klettenberg Park before school, but he still went every afternoon, immediately school was over – and in Germany school stops at lunchtime. If he had training at five o'clock with FC Cologne, his knees were green by the time he showed up. Lars made huge progress almost immediately after he switched clubs, but that had less to do with FC Cologne than it did with the vagaries of puberty. He grew a foot in a year. Before his 15th birthday he was already six foot four inches tall.

To a child's logic, an invitation from FC Cologne to be a goalkeeper was the highest honour you could get. Among the professionals of FC Cologne in the early eighties was Toni Schumacher, one of the best goalkeepers in the world, so that meant that as an FC youth keeper you would be just as good within a few years. Didn't it?

Once, during training, Lars ran impetuously out of his goal. He hadn't a chance of catching the cross, and his fist collided not with the ball but with the head of Günther Baerhausen – incidentally, a player who really would become a professional, in the Zweite Bundesliga with VfL Osnabrück.

'Who do you think you are – Toni Schumacher?' shouted Baerhausen.

'I'm just trying to get the cross,' Lars called back, and that meant: Yes, of course I think I'm the new Schumacher.

That conviction still hadn't left him when he turned 16. He *knew* he was the next Schumacher. So it was hardly what you would call a well-planned decision when one autumnal Monday Lars suddenly stopped going to training with the under-16s. It was the result of a brainstorm, done on an adolescent whim. The previous day they had drawn against Alemannia Aachen. For a youth team used to winning by five or six goals to nil it was tantamount to a defeat. At Geissbockheim – as FC Cologne's ground is known, because of the billy-goat, or *Geissbock*, on the club badge – their coach Roland Koch, who would later coach the professionals of VfB Stuttgart and Bayer Leverkusen, had told them that their training was going to get tougher. Lars had felt personally wounded. He just wanted to do the right thing. Wasn't it enough that his girlfriend Claudia, the first girlfriend he had ever had, was always teasing him for never thinking of anything but his bloody football? And now he was being insulted on the football field as well.

Something just clicked – you can all go fuck yourselves. You think the whole world's against you. OK, fine, then you'll stand up to the whole world. So the day after the Aachen game I didn't go to training, without thinking that was me finished with football. I

just thought, I'm not going. Instead I went to the pictures with my girlfriend. And the next weekend as well, to a proper disco for the first time; those were things there was hardly any time for because I always had to train four or five times a week. Then I thought, 'You see, you were right not to go to training.' All hell broke loose at FC Cologne. What was up? Why wasn't I coming? The parents of team-mates rang up, Koch came to my house, but he got all psychological about it – he understood everything and so on. Maybe I just needed someone to give me a good bollocking, I don't know. Deep in my heart I wanted to start training again; I was already regretting my rebellion even while I was still rebelling. But I couldn't admit it. I became defiant – I'm through with football, leave me alone – and at some point, probably sooner than I would have liked, they actually did leave me in peace. They'd written me off. FC Cologne under-16s got themselves a new goalkeeper, and that was that.

It was the end of a professional career, before it had even begun. Lars didn't have the time to grieve, or even to have regrets. His weeks started to follow a new rhythm. Instead of training, training, training, it was now Monday the cinema, Tuesday *Dallas* and Wednesday *Dynasty* – sitting with his girlfriend in front of the television watching American soaps. After a few weeks Claudia was alone again while watching *Dallas*. Lars was sitting with her mother in the sitting-room, watching the highlights of the European Cup games on the second television.

It was the only period in Lars' life when he didn't play football. After three or four months he realised what he was missing: not necessarily the chance to be a professional, not so much the feeling of playing for FC Cologne, but the camaraderie of a team.

After the summer holidays, nine months after he walked out on FC Cologne, he picked up his sports bag and went to BC Efferen. It was the nearest club. What division they played in, and Efferen's youth team was in the second from the bottom, was of secondary importance. That feeling of happiness when you've won, when you've won *together*, that was what Lars was after. You can get that with any side.

Some people in Efferen recognised him as the former FC Cologne under-16 goalkeeper. They thought it was fantastic that they were getting such a good goalkeeper.

'No,' Lars corrected then, 'I'm going to be playing in midfield.'

Of course it occurred to him that he'd thrown away his professional career. When, in 1988, after a home game, the professionals of FC Cologne did a lap of honour in the Müngersdorf Stadium – and at the time they more often had cause to do that than they would a few years later – Lars was standing, as he did at almost every game, in the South End wearing his FC scarf. He applauded when the players ran past, Ralf Sturm among them. Three years earlier he and Lars had played together at Geissbockheim. Lars went on applauding, yelling with excitement, but at the same time it hurt. At least gloomy 'that might have been me' thoughts like that came only in short flashes.

I was doing OK. I had my team in Efferen, and on Friday evenings we all went to the Lantern, that's this pub in Hürth, and drank. On Saturday evening too we all went together to the Lantern, but no one, not a single one of us, drank anything stronger than Coke. Thirteen hearty young men sipping lemonades

on a Saturday evening and talking about hardly anything but their game the following afternoon. In the Kreisliga. But that was our world. I have a friend who says he could never be in a team, he'd go mad if he had to conform and adapt. With me it was always the other way round. I always liked that togetherness. I liked it when someone told me, 'You'll be there at such and such a time. We need you.'

And he made sure he turned up at ten o'clock on the dot one Saturday morning in July 1989 in Bettgenhausen-Seelbach, for Josef Engert needed him. Engert had formerly worked as a caretaker on the housing estate in Hürth, and he remembered that Frau Leese's tall son had been a goal-keeper with FC Cologne. Now he lived in the Westerwald, Engert said, and a few of his friends urgently needed a keeper for the Schoppenturnier, or 'pint tournament', in Seelbach. These friendly events were so-called because local pubs would each put up a team. One other reason, though, is that many of the players downed pints at half-time.

When newspaper reporters write profiles of sportsmen, they like to write about turning points in their careers, those moments when chance and a little bit of luck put a player on the right track. As a 13-year-old defender with SC Munich 06, Franz Beckenbauer was thumped by an opponent of the same age playing for TSV 1860 Munich, so in 1958 he went to Bayern instead of 1860. Twelve-year-old Cassius Clay's new Schwinn bicycle was stolen in Louisville in 1954; the policeman who took his statement advised him to stop crying and become a boxer. Lars Leese was invited to the darkest corner of the Westerwald by a former care-taker to take part in a tournament that some people played while half-drunk. Without Engert's phone call Lars might still be playing midfield for BC Efferen.

Normally the goalkeepers at such tournaments are between the sticks because they are 47 years old and carrying 20 stone, so it isn't difficult to imagine the impression made by a six-foot-five-inch 19-year-old, one whose arms were unusually thin (Lars weighed about 15 stone) but also unusually purposeful. When they were all sitting together over a beer on their last evening, some of the players still in their kit, Lars' team-mates took the cup they had won and filled it with money. 'Take it back to Cologne,' they said. He counted 350 marks, or just over £100. He felt dizzy. Because of the money, certainly – after all, he was still a schoolboy – but more than anything because he was touched by the gesture.

It was while Lars was enjoying the victory celebrations that one of the pint-footballers, Uwe Fritzchen, asked him if he fancied playing for his club, Sportfreunde Neitersen.

Rudolf Bellersheim heard about this later, in the Laatsch pizzeria, Neitersen's only pub. They'd had a fantastic goal-keeper at the pint tournament in Seelbach, Fritzchen said, and he wanted to play for Neitersen.

'Is that right? And where does he come from?' asked Bellersheim.

'Cologne.'

'Cologne? Have you lost your marbles?'

'No,' said Fritzchen. 'He likes it here in the Westerwald and he wants to come. And he is a former FC youth goal-keeper.' He might have said he was a former international youth player, but Bellersheim can't quite remember now.

'Fine, bring him over,' said Bellersheim.

'He's going to be another fly-by-night,' thought Emil Sojka, the Neitersen coach, when he heard of the arrival of this fantastic goalkeeper. Sojka already had three keepers in his squad. None of them was so good that you would say he needn't ever look out for another one, but, to be honest, as a coach in the Kreisliga Sojka didn't exactly expect that anyone much better would cross his path. And what he had heard about the new recruit seemed to tell him everything he needed to know: he hadn't played in goal for three years. 'You have to be careful with people like that,' said Sojka. 'You have to ask, "Why hasn't he been playing? Is he a troublemaker?"' Some other people were more enthusiastic than the coach. Club chairman Bellersheim made a point of coming to training, and Jochen Rosbach, who was still coaching the reserve team at the time but who was to take over the first team from Sojka after seven matches, was waiting excitedly for a first-class striker. Somewhere along the line he had got the wrong end of the stick. 'I couldn't believe my eyes when Fritzchen yelled, "There he is!", and there was Lars in his goalie's kit,' Rosbach recalled. 'Why a goalkeeper? I wondered, disheartened.'

And then they all watched – Rosbach from the other half of the field, where he was training with the reserve team, Bellersheim from the sidelines, and, inevitably, a few yards away from him, Lars' friend Holger – as Sojka, 45 at the time but still with a footballer's physique (and the hairdo to go with it: blow-waved pony-tail and grey hair down the back of his neck) put Lars to the test. At least that's what Lars was expecting: he was utterly baffled by what Sojka actually did. He just threw the ball to him. Then he tried a few shots, either straight at Lars or very close to him so that he never really had to dive. After a dozen shots Sojka left the field, went over to Bellersheim and said, 'We'll take him.'

They called it a trial. A Kreisliga trial! Then, when the coach started kicking easy balls straight at me, I thought, 'Just how bad does he think I am?' And after perhaps ten shots, none of which I even had to stretch for, it was all over. It makes me laugh to think about it now. On the other hand, if you have an eye for it, you actually can see after ten shots whether someone's any good. Or at least good enough for the Kreisliga. There, some goalies hit themselves in the eye when they try to catch the ball.

In Neitersen, Lars ignored the fact that the role of the goalkeeper is essentially a passive one, and led and directed from the back row. Never again as a goalkeeper would he have such an influence on his team's style of play. Normally, a goalkeeper reacts. He has to wait until the other team's striker comes towards him and for his defenders to make a play before he does anything. Lars refused to wait. He was proactive. Often he would play 20 yards away from his goal, outside the penalty area – a goalkeeper's natural habitat; he regularly came 12 or 13 yards off his goal-line to deal with crosses – a defender's natural habitat. Lars created his own position: he was a goalkeeper–libero–coach.

And he loved it.

There is little as important to Lars as the feeling of being liked by everyone, so he tried to be the leader and team clown all in one. When the opposing team arrived in Neitersen, he would stand on the dressing-room bench, his face pressed to the half-open window, and yell, 'What do you think you're doing here, you piss-artists? We'll eat you for breakfast!' It was supposed to be funny, but it was also supposed to be serious. On his way out of the dressing-room he would hammer on the opposing team's door and shout, 'Come out, you lot, stop chattering. Come on, are you scared or what?' After the match he would go over, all gentle and friendly, and offer the other team's players a beer. You've got to understand that he was a different person before and after the match, he says. He generally won the admiration not only of his team-mates but of his opponents as well.

On one occasion, though, he went too far. Every goal-keeper has swung out with his fist in a penalty-area mêlée while trying to clear a ball, or rammed his knee into a striker's back; that's how goalkeepers mark their territory. But something else was going on when Lars ran up to striker Uwe Krämer during a home game against SG Langenhahn after the visitors had scored and kicked his legs out from under him. Krämer flew three feet into the air. There was one hell of a fuss. Krämer had trodden on his hands, Lars roared. Krämer's team-mates tried to collar him, his team-mates tried to protect him, and spectators ran on to the field. But the referee hadn't seen a thing. The game continued, and the goalkeeper went unpunished.

When I phoned Rosbach in Neitersen for the first time and got through to the vicar's office, I assumed I'd dialled a wrong number. The second time I called, it turned out that Rosbach is married to the vicar. I liked him at first sight. Even at the age of 59, his face radiates something childlike and gentle from under his silver hair. He recalled being frightened by the way Lars had hunted down Krämer. 'I knew Lars was round the bend,' Rosbach said. 'Fanatical on the pitch and a really nice guy once the game was over, I'd have to say he enriched my life. But I was horrified that he could let himself go like that.' Even today, 12 years later, Rosbach is still suffering as a result of Lars' loss of control that day. Uwe Krämer is now a referee in the Westerwald, and if he is in charge of a game with SG Altenkirchen, Rosbach's current side, he seldom hesitates to award a free-kick against his team. 'And I was only Lars' coach,' Rosbach added.

For all his many skills, there was one thing that Lars couldn't do: let in a goal. 'A goal by the opposition was the death penalty as far as he was concerned,' said Rosbach. 'He would kick the goal-post furiously, and then switch off. His commands to his team-mates stopped, he wasn't a hundred per cent involved any more; as far as he was concerned the game was over, even if we were leading 5–1. In his eyes he had lost because he had let that one goal through.'

And his fanaticism was infectious. During his second season with Neitersen three or four of the players would join him at the window shouting greetings to the opposing team, advising them to go home immediately. At the end of Lars' first season, Sportfreunde Neitersen had finished seventh of 14 teams, but now the whole team believed they were unbeatable – just as long as their goalkeeper wore the same underclothes for every game.

At that time they usually played on ashpits, so Lars wore cycling shorts under his long black goalkeeper's shorts as a second layer, with a comic figure called Genschman sewn on to them. The Frankfurt satirical magazine *Titanic* had introduced this flying figure into the world, a hybrid of Superman and German Foreign Minister Hans-Dietrich Genscher, with Genscher's trademark protruding ears. At some point, one of his team-mates learned that Lars believed these shorts guaranteed a win.

That was more or less how it started. Before every game someone would shout, 'Show us the Genschman shorts!' And I would open my sports bag and announce, 'Here they are again, the legendary

Genschman shorts!' Same thing every time. Then I would hold them in the air while everyone cheered. Most sportsmen are superstitious, even in the Bundesliga. At VfB Stuttgart the goalkeeping coach sits on the subs' bench at every match wearing the same shorts again, even if it's 15 degrees below and snowing. My mother knew not to wash the Genschman shorts at too high a temperature because they were in tatters: on no account could they fall to pieces. When I was warming up in Neitersen I always chose exactly the same spot on the field to do my exercises. If there was a puddle, then tough, I'd sit in the puddle. Stupid really, a superstition like that, when you think about it. You make yourself totally dependent. I would have to check ten times to make sure I'd packed the Genschman shorts. Today, after such a long time in football, I know that super-stition doesn't help, but even so, I'm still supersti-tious. Even when you know it's useless you still do it. Because you're living with the anxiety: what'll happen if you don't follow your superstition? Will that make you have a bad game?

In May 1991 Neitersen became champions of the Westerwald-Sieg Kreisliga, having lost only one game all season. 'By that time Lars really should have gone,' said Neitersen libero Jürgen Sanner, 'he was too good for us.' The idea had in fact occurred to Lars, but only vaguely. He would go *at some point*. For the time being it was enough for him to be considered the best goalkeeper from Daadetal to Atzelgift, to win almost every Sunday, and to play in a team that shared his obsession, his enthusiasm and even his superstition.

Only Georg Roezel, the manager of VfB Wissen, was able to persuade Lars to leave Neitersen, and he wouldn't call until six months later. Roezel kept it brief. 'We want you,' he said.

Wissen were the best team in the Westerwald. They were among the top teams in the Oberliga, with only (at that time) the two Bundesliga divisions above them. This was a different enticement altogether from the usual requests. In February 1992, Lars told his coach Jochen Rosbach that after three years with Sportfreunde Neitersen he was going to switch to VfB Wissen when the season ended. Until then, his Sundays in Neitersen would remain more or less unchanged. Now they were in the Bezirksliga, Neitersen no longer won every game, but they were happy to settle for mid-table obscurity.

Sportfreunde Neitersen were relegated from the Bezirksliga the following season. It was mostly because they had lost their goalkeeper, said coach Jochen Rosbach. But in a way Lars Leese never left Neitersen. 'Every time the other side scored, you'd hear it again: "Lars would have stopped that one; that wouldn't have happened with Lars,"' said Rosbach. 'I'd have to say that every goalkeeper after him here got a really rough deal, because they were always being compared with Lars. One of his successors, Herbert Wagner, once shouted, "If I hear the name Lars Leese one more time, I'm out of here!"'

2

'I'M PREGNANT'

DANIELA HESS CAME home from a match on 12 February 1994 and told her diary that she was in love. It's a good thing diaries can't ask questions, because if hers had – Who was the boy? What was he like? – she wouldn't have had much of an answer. How was she supposed to know? She'd never exchanged so much as a word with him. All she knew about him was the way he leapt at crosses, the way he hurled himself at shots, the way he waited for the ball and the opponent. 'He had this way of standing there that was all his own,' said Daniela, 'not completely upright, but then again not crouching down as low as many other goal-keepers. It was somewhere in between: bent slightly forwards, his bodyweight balanced on his toes, and his torso swaying left and right, not backwards and forwards.' That vision was enough to make her split up with Thorsten, the boy she had been going out with for five years. For some time, she hadn't quite been sure whether or not she still loved him, but now she knew: she loved the man with the slightly bent posture and his weight balanced on his toes.

Things like that are always happening in movies – it's called love at first sight – but the fact that it was really happening confused Daniela Hess. Daniela was 20 years old and had brown curly hair; she was a dental assistant in the town of Gelnhausen, not far from Frankfurt. As she tried to put her feelings in order on her way back from that football match in the Oberliga Südwest between VfB Wissen and TSG Pfeddersheim, she suddenly started crying.

'What's wrong now?' asked Stefan Simm, who played as a defender with VfB Wissen and had been delighted at first that one of his friends had finally agreed to accompany him on the 150-kilometre journey from his home in eastern Hesse into the Westerwald. But he hadn't expected Daniela to end up in floods of tears.

'The keeper,' she said.

'He's got a girlfriend,' said Simm.

It made no difference.

'Say hi from me anyway.'

'I'm supposed to say hi from Danny.'

'What? Who?' asked Lars Leese in the dressing-room the following Monday as he and Stefan were getting ready for their first training session of the week.

'You don't know her, but she saw you on Saturday,' Simm explained.

'Ah,' said Lars. 'Well then, say hi from me too.'

And that was enough on that subject. When training began, Lars didn't give this unknown girl another thought. And he wouldn't for the next three months. There was too much else to brood on and talk about: football; and football; and football. At the time, Lars was working for the SHP computer company in Hürth. He shared an office with a female colleague, but he forgot all about her too whenever

Matthias Becker, his closest friend on the Wissen team, phoned him. They'd run through everything: who the good players were on the next team they were up against, which of them had played badly the previous Sunday, how many matches they still needed to win. And then they'd go back to the beginning and do it all over again.

VfB Wissen, a club from a small town outside Siegen, about 75 kilometres east of Bonn, with only 9,000 inhabitants, were exceeding everyone's expectations. With effect from August 1994, the German Football Association planned to introduce a semi-professional Regionalliga, sandwiched between the Oberliga and the two Bundesliga divisions. The idea was that traditionally big clubs such as Arminia Bielefeld, FC Nürnberg and Hannover 96, all of whom had been relegated from professional football in recent years, would not fall as hard when pushed out of the Zweite Bundesliga as they'd formerly done. And now the village club VfB Wissen was well on its way to that league. Six teams from Oberliga Südwest were allowed into this new so-called Dritte Liga, or third division, and so that no small club which happened to have had an unusually good year could qualify, the results for the two most recent years were factored in. To everyone's surprise, in 1992/93, Lars' first season with Wissen, the club had come fifth in their league. In the spring of 1994, as the 1993/94 season was entering its crucial phase, once again the villagers were defiantly up in the top group.

It was their coach, Elmar Müller, who had put them there, Lars was quite sure of that. Müller got more out of his players than they thought was there in the first place. 'What a guy!' Lars thought, but he wasn't entirely certain whether he meant that in a good way. The wristband clip on Müller's watch had sprung open 20 times during his introductory speech in Wissen, as many times as he had thumped his right fist into his left hand. A tough-looking Westphalian with a full, round face, dark curly hair and a deep voice, Müller was quite capable of talking himself into a fury: *he* had coached Preussen Münster, and *they* would have to work harder, run harder, play harder, talk harder, kick harder, scratch harder, sing harder in the shower. And then, simple as that, they'd be more successful. At the end of such speeches there was always silence – in a room packed with 24 people. Whenever Lars looked at his team-mates he'd see that their faces were completely frozen.

And now the 1993/94 season really did seem to be drawing to a close with qualification for the Regionalliga. A massive marquee had already been set up in the meadow below the sports field in Wissen in time for the last match of the season against Borussia Neunkirchen on 14 May. On the day, more than 2,000 spectators turned up. Both clubs needed only a draw for promotion.

Daniela Hess had borrowed a friend's car because she no longer trusted her old Ford Fiesta to make the journey from Gelnhausen to the Westerwald. Two other friends of Stefan Simm's were with her. They'd heard something to the effect that she didn't just want to go to Wissen because of the party that was planned, but because there was some goalkeeper or other involved as well. Daniela hadn't seen him since that game three months earlier, but that didn't matter. She had an image of him in her head, the tall, thin, fair-haired man with the slightly bent crouching posture; she projected her love on to that. To be happy, sometimes you need only love in your mind. The first footballer she had loved was the international Karlheinz Riedle when she was 16. And she only knew him from the football stickers they used to swap at school.

What a disappointment it was, then, to see the goalkeeper playing against Neunkirchen. All of a sudden he looked quite different. In April Lars had torn a ligament in his thigh, and the Nigerian reserve keeper Angus Ikeji had taken his place. But Lars could still run fast enough to get into the picture when the final whistle blew: in the victory photograph published in the *Rhein-Zeitung* the following Monday, he's right in the middle, even though he'd only been watching. The game had ended – what a surprise, when both teams needed a draw – goalless. The party in the tent was already under way after the 50th minute of play.

'And all at once Lars was sitting beside me in the beer tent,' said Daniela.

There was loud music coming out of the speakers.

'Are you the one who said hi?' asked Lars.

The table in front of them was wobbling. Four or five men were jumping up and down on it. They called it dancing.

Yes, she was, said Daniela.

Further off in the tent someone shouted 'Watch out!' and everyone jumped aside. A glass tipped over and beer slopped over the wooden table.

'That was very nice of you, thanks – but why?' asked Lars.

The men on the table roared: 'Wissen for the cup!'

We don't need to reproduce much more of their conversation, Lars reckons: 'It was the way parties are. There's laughing, dancing, snogging.' In any case, Daniela thought that the most important thing had already been said pretty quickly between them – not in words, not even directly in glances. It was just clear, just like that. 'We both knew neither of us would be going home alone that night.'

And sure enough they went home together – with Stefan Simm. Neither Daniela nor Lars had a place to stay in the Westerwald, so they ended up in Simm's studio flat. Daniela and Lars were in his bed, while the host lay on the sofa ten feet away. The next afternoon they parted, Daniela feeling she had found love, Lars convinced that he'd had a pleasant evening.

Promotion to the Western Regionalliga convinced everyone at VfB Wissen that they were finally in the big time. You only had to look at the list of the teams they were due to play: Arminia Bielefeld, Rot-Weiss Essen, Alemannia Aachen, Preussen Münster. There would even be ball-boys in the stadium. Nobody mentioned little clubs such as Hauenstein, Edenkoben and Bocholt, their other less distinguished opponents. People noticed you when you were in the Regionalliga. 'Oh, really? You're playing there?' said Lars' friends in Cologne, and he thought, 'Now you've made something of yourself.'

When the feeling of vertigo from the new surroundings had subsided, VfB Wissen seriously set about turning themselves into a great team, or at least into something that people thought was a great team. The management committee said it could put up a budget of a million marks (over £300,000), which wasn't worth mentioning in comparison to Bielefeld (4.2 million marks/£1.4 million) or Rot-Weiss Essen (3.6 million marks £1.2 million), but for a small-town club it was huge money. The players were to receive expenses of between 1,000 and 10,000 marks (about £325 to £3,250) a month, they spent a week in a training camp in Seefeld in Austria, and in Wissen stadium new grass would be laid and the grandstand would be renovated to seat 12,700 spectators – more people than lived in Wissen. And to ensure that everything looked properly professional, a loyal club member, Sepp Becker, was immediately appointed press spokesman.

But where the details were concerned, things weren't perhaps quite as professional as they might have been. When the team lost its first Regionalliga game against SC Verl 4–1, coach Müller raged that it hadn't exactly been fantastic 'sitting for hours at 90 degrees in a bus like an oven on the way here'. What he didn't say was that the bus had actually had air conditioning but he'd ordered it to be switched off so that the players could get used to the heat. Sepp Becker, the press spokesman, issued his first statement: 'The Verl team covered twice as much ground as we did!' The game was just as much of a learning curve for Lars. He had started well, with two saves in the first five minutes, but later in the match he hadn't lived up to that early promise, especially with Verl's second goal when he stayed on his goal-line and failed to clear a cross that Verl's striker, Angelo Vier, headed easily into the net.

On the Monday before training, Müller summoned the team to the dressing-room for a match analysis. As always, he was wearing football boots and a tracksuit, although he never played. When they were travelling on the bus he liked to roll his tracksuit trousers up over his knees and sprint up and down in the service-station car park, saying to himself: 'Here we go, here we go!' This time, in the dressing-room, he had zipped his tracksuit all the way to the top and pulled the collar up to his chin. He stared at Lars. Müller acted as though he was trying to make himself heard by a deaf person in a hurricane.

'For the second goal you didn't come off your line and when the third goal went in I don't even know where you were. In the toilet?' roared the coach.

'I was lying on the ground trying to get my breath back because someone kicked me in the kidneys,' Lars defended himself, or tried to.

'Bollocks – no one saw that!' yelled Müller.

'The ref would have blown for a foul if he'd seen it,' said Lars.

'What are you on about? Things are tougher in the Regionalliga, you just have to grit your teeth and get on with it.'

The next Saturday, the coach put Angus Ikeji in goal. With the score standing at 1–1 against Alemannia Aachen, Ikeji let the ball slip through his fingers. The mistake cost Wissen the game. That was bound to send Müller into a fury. 'No, no,' says Müller today. 'You see, you have to trust a goalkeeper, you can't just take him off the first time he slips up.'

Lars found himself on the subs' bench until the tenth game of the season. Whether it really would have been much more satisfying to play is questionable: VfB started their first season in the Regionalliga with three wretched draws and six defeats. Could it be that the big wide world was just a bit too big for Wissen?

One Tuesday evening during this period, when Lars' only participation in the world of sport was as a spectator, his phone rang.

It was Daniela Hess.

Lars had visited her twice since the party to celebrate the team's promotion. They spoke often on the phone, and Daniela was aware 'that I felt more for him than he did for me'. It was still only a close friendship, but she noted with fascination 'how settled a character Lars was by then. I don't mean where women were concerned, of course. But in other respects he was: he went to work, to football training, to bed. It was all so orderly. On the other hand, I was living a life of carefree chaos. I bunked off work on Friday if I'd got plastered in a club on the Thursday. When I was 20 I barely gave a thought to the next day.'

Daniela asked Lars whether he fancied dropping by and seeing her at the weekend after his next match. She had something she wanted to discuss with him.

'What's up? You're not pregnant, are you?'

Lars laughed at his own joke; Daniela burst into tears.

Just that morning she'd still been able to say 'Ha ha, very

funny' when her doctor in Gelnhausen revealed to her that she was pregnant. Daniela had gone to his surgery when she suddenly started having sharp back pains at work. On Saturdays she played handball; perhaps, she'd thought, she'd been hit in the back. She couldn't really remember. 'Look, here's the ultrasound picture,' her doctor had said. 'There you can see the head, here are the legs, all properly formed. You're in your fourth month.'

All the thoughts that went hurtling through Daniela Hess's head were suppressed by a single one: 'This won't do, I'm going to have to have an abortion.' She was pregnant by the man she was trying to convince herself to forget about. She knew Lars had another girlfriend, that he didn't really want to be with her; otherwise they'd have settled down ages ago. In desperation she drove to Hanau to see her friend Sabine. At the motorway junction she should have braked to get in lane behind a lorry; instead she put her foot on the accelerator. 'I kept it there, that's all I can remember. I don't know if the lorry accelerated, or if he let me pull in ahead of him; I only know I somehow made it to Sabine's.'

From there she tried to call Lars. She dialled, put the phone down, dialled, put the phone down, dialled again. Then Sabine said, 'If you don't get on with it I'm going to thump you!'

'What do you mean you're in your fourth month?' asked Lars, interrupting the sobbing at the other end of the line.

'I'm in my fourth month, and this week I'm going to Holland with Sabine to have an abortion.'

'Listen: you have the child and I'll bring it up,' said Lars. He just wanted to say something comforting.

I had a big mouth. Of course that isn't how you imagine it's going to be, becoming a father. But to some

extent I was prepared for it. Somehow it would be OK. Somehow everything's always OK. Everything has its positive side, I really believe that. In that situation I had to look for the positive for a while, true enough, and then I said to myself, 'Cool, you're going to be a young father.' The worst thing was introducing myself to Danny's parents. They didn't even know me. I felt as though I was going for a job interview. I put on my best shirt and a pair of proper trousers, but no tie. A tie, I thought, would have made me look too guilty. I was totally terrified. You imagine everything – that they're going to go for your throat or whatever – and then after everything it was a really pleasant afternoon. 'Make the best of it,' Danny's father said to me. There were no accusations, just nice supportive words. Then I even went and played tennis with him. While we're warming up he tries to get a lob past me, but I get to it and smash the ball – right between her father's eyes. He went over like a sack. My heart stood still. Panicking, I watched him slowly get to his feet. He was dazed, but smiling. What a relief: he was smiling.

Early in November, Lars became Wissen's first-choice goal-keeper again, but the team wasn't doing any better. VFB WISSEN IN INTENSIVE CARE the *Rhein-Zeitung* reported after a 4–1 loss at the hands of Preussen Münster. For two months the players got only crumbs of the incomes they'd been promised. During training, coach Müller noticed, 'They only talked about money. "Have you had anything?"' At that point the club's debts had supposedly risen to 500,000 marks – more than £150,000. Klaus Schwamborn, the committee chairman, resigned, and the members were happy to accept the reason he gave: heart problems. The supporters were asked to make donations, but things got off to a poor start: the *Rhein-Zeitung* published the wrong telephone number and account details. But there were other reasons why not enough money came in. A club that rarely had more than 2,500 and now barely had 1,000 spectators could hardly hope to persuade its supporters to come up with half a million marks.

Now that the enthusiasm about Regionalliga status had faded, everyone claimed to have known all along that it was bound to end in bankruptcy. How in the world had they imagined they would be able to come up with a budget of a million marks? Like all other clubs in the league, they got 175,000 marks from broadcasters ARD for the television rights; in addition, they could safely anticipate 350,000 marks before tax from takings at the gate. Which came to 525,000 marks. And the rest? Pudy would sort it out. That summer, in the marquee, to the sound of loud music, they really had believed that. For a long time the team had been relying on Wolfgang Pudich, their director. On occasion, Pudy came to the games in his 120,000-mark (£40,000) Lotus Omega with his trouser pockets bursting with cash. In November 1994, however, his central-heating empire was in financial trouble. It was plain that he wouldn't be able to help VfB.

Lars had worked out that he could earn between 2,000 and 3,000 marks (up to £1,000) a month playing Regionalliga football. He bought himself a black open-top Ford Escort for 35,000 marks (£11,500). Before he had the money. His bank loan had to be paid back in monthly instalments of 1,000 marks (£350), and it was easy to predict that rather than the 3,000 marks he was hoping for, for the rest of the season he was likely to get 500 marks (£175) from Wissen, as he had done in September and October. Lars didn't need a pocket calculator to work out that it wouldn't be enough. Monthly income: 1,900 marks (£675) net from job with the computer company SHP, 500 marks from VfB Wissen = 2,400 marks (£850). Monthly outgoings: 960 marks (£325) for rent and heating, 1,000 marks (£350) for loan repayments, 400 marks (£150) for petrol for 20 round trips from Cologne to Wissen, 290 marks (£100) for car insurance = 2,650 marks (£925). And that was before he ate or drank anything.

I've often thought to myself: 'You go to work five days a week and then you're training, you get home at half past ten, you play football on Saturday, and you can't even get ten marks out of the cashpoint. How does that happen?' But I'm not the kind of person who goes around saying, 'I'm having a really crap time of it.' Instead I've tended to stand another round, thinking, 'Regionalliga player, double income, they expect it of you.' I didn't want to draw attention to it particularly. After all, I was Lars Leese, the golden boy. As far as the club was concerned, people were always saying, 'OK, something'll come in next week,' and then I'd go back to the bank all smiles. 'Next week you'll get my credit payment.' And then once again nothing came from VfB. But you haven't the courage to go to the bank and tell them. You wait till they phone you, and that makes everything twice as bad. At the end of the Regionalliga season I was 30,000 marks (about £10,000) in debt, with the bank, with my friends, all over the place.

During the winter break, coach Elmar Müller was fired. It was just a weary act of duty – *something* had to be done. Wolfgang Rausch, an elegant, down-to-earth man who had played with Bayern Munich, took over the team. He quickly realised that it was no longer a question of drawing up tactical master plans. First of all he had to persuade players who had neither won nor been paid for months to show a bit of commitment. Rausch tried to achieve this by identifying someone every Monday as Twat of the Week. For the rest of the week a player who had been particularly twattish would have to wear a yellow shirt. There had to be *something* to laugh at.

The new coach adapted the style of play to the state of the club: minimal risk for minimal payment. Wissen restricted themselves to defence, unfortunately with minimal success. In Rausch's first game in charge they struggled to stay at 0–0; as soon as Wissen conceded a goal, they fell apart.

At times like that, with teams like that, a goalkeeper is all on his own. Exposed to attack after attack, abandoned by his resigned defenders, Lars effectively took refuge in that loneliness; he no longer judged games according to their results, just according to his own performance. A 3–0 defeat against Preussen Cologne was a tolerable result because the *Kölner Stadt-Anzeiger* confirmed for him: 'It was only Leese who stopped things getting any worse.' After a 5–0 thrashing by TuS Paderborn it wasn't hard for him to tell *kicker* sport magazine 'We really got slaughtered' because, thanks to a penalty save and a few other good stops, he didn't have to include himself in that *we*. Sportsmen are only team-players when they win. Lars was no exception. In the second half of the season he was enough of an egoist to take some comfort from his new role – the best man in the worst team.

But on Tuesday, 21 March 1995, he ran off the pitch in the middle of training. The groundsman was waving frantically at him: 'Lars! Lars!' A phone call: Fräulein Hess had gone into labour at the hospital. Two hours later the goalkeeper was in the clinic in Gelnhausen.

'Where is Danny? Is she already in the delivery room?' he asked when he saw her father in the hospital entrance.

'She's over there,' her father said.

Lars had run straight past her. He hadn't recognised her.

The last time he had seen her had been a good ten weeks previously, which had given Daniela time to worry about the lack of interest he was showing in her and their child. 'It was the first time I'd thought: "So he's not as great as he thinks he is."'

During Lars' last visit she had weighed about nine stone, and her face still had its girlish features. The only visible sign of her pregnancy was the beginning of a little belly. Now she weighed 12 stone and was sitting in a plastic chair in the yellow light of the hospital corridor. From her knees to her ankles her legs were fat, white tree-trunks. Her calves were unrecognisable. Water retention had swollen them up into elephants' feet. There was a danger that the child would be poisoned by all that water in the tissue, and its heart could barely be heard, the obstetrician had told her that Tuesday. He had sent her to the hospital to have the birth induced immediately.

By Thursday evening nothing had happened. Lars went home. He had a meeting at work, an important customer who wanted to place an order, and he told Daniela, 'If I don't make it, they'll throw me out.' On Friday afternoon at five to one he was back in Gelnhausen. He had missed the birth of his daughter Vivian by ten minutes.

On the journey I had this feeling: 'You're going to just miss it.' On a car journey like that you have far too much time to brood, and you invent the stupidest scenarios for yourself. But holding a child in your hands ten minutes after the birth isn't much worse

than right after the birth – or at least that's what I think now. To be honest, I have one image in my mind above all, because Danny has gone on about it so much and described it so many times: I'm holding Vivian in the palm of my hand, and we're just looking at each other, quite still, deep in each other's eyes, she, this little monkey weighing five pounds, and me, the big tall giant. It had been clear for ages that I wasn't going to bring up the child as I'd offered – Danny had built up far too strong a relationship with the baby during her pregnancy. After the birth she came to see me in Cologne every few weeks. At the time I had a little two-room flat in Ehrenfeld, and then, a year after we first met, a year after we'd conceived a child, we got to know each other. I mean, really got to know each other. There was nothing there, we didn't love each other, but we were the best of friends. We talked through the night, we talked about everything really.

'Except about us,' says Daniela. 'We talked about sport, films, the best way to rinse the dishes, other people's love affairs, but we avoided talking about what we felt about each other. I was afraid he would notice that I was still in love. Yeah, and then there was the business about the christening.'

About a dozen friends and relations assembled in the little flat in Ehrenfeld for a private party after the ceremony. The previous tenant had built a proper bar in the sitting-room, and most of the guests huddled around it until the evening. Lars, however, left the party in his own flat early. He said he was going to a restaurant with his football team.

The next morning he hadn't come back. Out of her mind

with worry, Daniela called his office number. Lars said he'd stayed over with his girlfriend.

'Your girlfriend? What girlfriend? I didn't know you had a girlfriend again!' Daniela shouted.

'Yeah, I do.'

'And you've nothing better to do than vanish from your daughter's christening and spend the night with a girlfriend you've never even mentioned to me? I'm going home, and you're never going to see me again.'

'I won't stand in your way,' said Lars defiantly.

With the furious intention of leaving not a trace of Vivian behind in Lars' flat, Daniela packed her bags and set off. It couldn't go on like this. Under those circumstances she didn't want to see Lars any more.

Lars had always thought he was a lucky kind of person. He still did. The fight with Daniela, the debts, relegation with VfB Wissen from the Regionalliga after a measly four victories in 34 matches – of course, if you looked at it like that it wasn't exactly brilliant. But it would never have occurred to Lars to see it like that. He was someone who was always lucky, that was just how things were. OK, not right now, but basically he was lucky. Or he soon would be.

In the summer of 1995, after six years in the Westerwald, Lars was back in Cologne playing for SC Preussen in the Oberliga. It was something of a demotion, but after that year in Wissen was each new beginning not a kind of promotion? He was 26 and he didn't have any special expectations, nothing crazy or unrealistic – he wasn't presumptuous that way.

'What does good luck mean for you?' he was asked in the fanzine *Preussen Power*.

'Not having bad luck,' he replied.

3

PROFESSIONAL FOOTBALLER?

L ARS' CONVICTION THAT he was lucky was confirmed when his employer SHP went bust and he was immediately taken on by the building materials company Raab-Karcher. He worked as an IT buyer in the Bonn branch. He liked the job. He had an office of his own and enough time to play card-games on his computer. Mostly he was on the phone, often talking to football colleagues from Preussen Cologne or to computer manufacturers, issuing orders, listening to offers. Lars loved talking. He was delighted every time the phone rang in his office.

'Hello, Rettig here from Bayer Leverkusen.'

'Hello, how can I help you?' Lars didn't went to risk saying the man's name, because he wasn't sure he'd heard it properly. Rettich? There was nothing worse than addressing a customer by the wrong name.

'Herr Calmund would like to see you,' said Rettig. 'When would you have a moment?'

'In five or ten minutes?'

Lars wanted to shout. He had worked out his misunderstanding in a fraction of a second, and something like an electric shock had coursed through his body. Calmund? Bayer Leverkusen? They didn't want to sell computers, they wanted him!

'Look,' Lars finally said, 'I'm sure Herr Calmund's diary is much fuller than mine. When would it suit you?'

It was December 1995, the winter break, so there was no training. He had time in the evening after work.

'Come by the stadium in two days' time, on Wednesday at six. Give your name at reception and ask for me: Rettig.'

'Yes, of course, Herr Rettig,' said Lars. Now he'd understood the name – if nothing else.

Bayer Leverkusen, one of the best clubs in the German Bundesliga, wanted me. But why? For their reserve team, which played in the North Rhine Oberliga, like Preussen Cologne, or for the professionals? I hadn't dared to ask Rettig. I didn't even know who Rettig was. But if I was to go to Calmund, the general manager of the Bundesliga team, that meant that Bayer wanted to take me on as a professional. What would Calmund say to me? Surely he wouldn't just show up with an offer of a contract? Oh, God! I had no idea how much money I should ask them for. What I needed was a cigarette.

However unexpected the call from the Bundesliga club might have been, Lars should really have been prepared for anything after his first five months with Preussen Cologne. In his first game he'd become aware that a good match for a city club and a win for Westerwald villagers are two quite different things. Lars thought the saves that had secured his team's 0–0 draw against Schwarz–Weiss Essen had been perfectly normal; after all, he'd played much like that for Wissen. But he quickly learned otherwise: what was seen as normal in the Westerwald, and therefore not worth mentioning, caused a bit of a hoo-ha in the city. 'Goalkeeper Lars Leese seems to be continuing the tradition of good goalkeepers with Preussen, and has wiped out all memories of Oliver Adler since his transfer to Oberhausen', wrote the *Kölner Stadt-Anzeiger* after watching him play for just 90 minutes. Lars thought to himself: 'Wow, to get accolades like that you'd have had to save like God almighty for three years in the Westerwald.'

A few months and several good matches later, Tony Woodcock, Preussen's coach, came over to him and said, 'Beanpole, I'm sure you're going to make it as a professional.' When Preussen's chairman Winfried Pütz proudly revealed in the autumn, 'I have contacts with Borussia Dortmund, I'll get you a trial with them,' the goalkeeper answered, 'Fine, off you go.' He had got used to the fanfares, and he enjoyed them, too, but he thought of himself as realistic. He had played very well during his time at Wissen and all he had had was an offer from Preussen; just because he played in Cologne, just because everything got hyped up a bit in the city, he wasn't suddenly a candidate for the Bundesliga. There was no need for anyone to pretend otherwise.

A few weeks later, early in December 1995, he went to the German champions Borussia Dortmund for a trial.

Was I really as good as they seemed to think I was in Cologne? Had my talents simply been hidden in the depths of the Westerwald? 'Oh, come on, stop daydreaming,' I told myself. Looked at with a cool head, the German champions weren't going to take on a 26-year-old from the Oberliga. I was too old,

I'd spent too long playing at too low a level. I went to Dortmund not to become a professional, but to enjoy the training. To stand on the pitch with great players like Stefan Klos, Kalle Riedle, Jürgen Kohler, with Toni Schumacher as goalkeeping coach. 'Lars,' I said to myself, 'just enjoy yourself.'

Lars' chief aim was to be first into the dressing-room before training, for he was scared of showing up when it was already full. How was he to greet the Borussia stars if they were completely naked? Was he supposed to shout 'good morning' to everyone, or go up to each individual, shake his hand and introduce himself: 'I'm Lars Leese, I've come from Preussen Cologne and I'm here for a trial'? And what if someone simply ignored his outstretched hand? Some Bundesliga professionals are supposed to be pretty arrogant. If he was first in he had nothing to worry about. The star players would simply have to come up to him or not, as they saw fit.

Forty-five minutes before the start of Lars' Dortmund trial, the players began to drift in. Most of them said hello to him, and that was that. Considering that they spend so much time in the public eye, many professional footballers are surprisingly shy of strangers. They speak when they are asked a question, but they aren't keen on initiating conversation themselves.

The previous day Borussia had played a European Cup match against Glasgow Rangers. Players who'd been in the line-up, like goalkeeper Stefan Klos, were trotting casually across the pitch. They were doing a bit of light running, nothing more. The minute he landed in the dressing-room, substitute goalkeeper Teddy de Beer complained that he hadn't had a wink of sleep all night. He wasn't going to train today, he was going to the gym. No one stood in his way, so Lars was alone with the goalkeeping coach, Toni

Schumacher. At the age of 13, Lars had stood behind the goal at the Geissbockheim Stadium and watched Schumacher training. Lars wanted to show him everything he could do, but that wasn't what Schumacher wanted.

The temperature was just above freezing, and the pitch was still solid from the night before. 'If I really put you to the test on the ground, you'll be out of action for a week,' said Schumacher. 'You've got to play for your team again on Saturday, so we'll take it easy for now.' He crossed a few balls into the penalty area, which Lars was supposed to punch away whatever height or angle they came at, and then there was a little game, five-a-side on a 35-metre field. Lars started getting into difficulties for the first time. How was he to call out instructions to the defenders? He couldn't yell at German internationals like Jürgen Kohler. He would have to get a hold of himself. 'You can't say, "Herr Kohler, if you have a moment would you mind passing to the striker to your left?' Lars said to himself, so he shouted, 'Behind you, on your left, Jürgen! On your left – your left, I said!'

Lars was doing well – or rather, like most novices who turn up for a trial with a professional team, he was happy he wasn't making any embarrassing mistakes. 'It certainly wasn't bad,' Schumacher said to him at the end. 'But I can't really tell from the little we've been able to do on the ground. Come back in the spring, and then we'll really see what you're made of.'

In Cologne they were less reticent, of course. SCHUMACHER ENTHUSIASTIC ABOUT LEESE proclaimed the *Kölnische Rundschau*. From Preussen chairman Pütz there was a Borussia pennant as a Christmas present.

Ten days later the call came from Andreas Rettig of Bayer Leverkusen.

*　　*　　*

'So what do I say if Calmund asks me about my wages, Heinz? I don't feel good about this,' said Lars. He was on the phone in his office again.

Heinz Rother, who played with Lars for Preussen, had once been a professional. Even if his career didn't look so great on the page – two years as a striker with FC Cologne, one Bundesliga game – Rother had been inside the business, he must know his way around it. But he didn't. It had been ten years since he had signed his contract as a professional footballer, and wages had changed since then. And in any case, Bayer Leverkusen paid quite different money from FC. How would Leverkusen want to sign Lars up anyway, as an amateur for the reserves or as a professional goalkeeper?

'I don't know, Heinz,' said Lars.

'You've just got to work out from what they say what their plans are for you,' advised Rother.

Lars' schoolfriend Holger Wacker, who was now working as an estate agent, suggested, 'Don't say a word about your wages. They want you, so they should put some numbers on the table.'

After recommendations like that, Lars didn't really feel properly equipped for a meeting with a wily Bundesliga general manager. Nervously, rather than with a cheerful sense of excitement, he drove to Leverkusen, to the Ulrich Haberland Stadium. He was picked up at reception by Rettig who – at least Lars had found this out in the meantime – was head of the youth academy. More importantly, though, he was Calmund's right-hand man.

Before he took him to meet the general manager, Rettig gave Lars the stadium tour – from the cell for hooligans to the professionals' spa pool. And Lars really listened, nervous as he was. For anyone who has watched Bundesliga games from the terraces, for anyone who imagines that being a professional footballer is simply a dream job, empty stadium catacombs aren't just sad pieces of concrete, they're a mythical kingdom. Every day hundreds of fans in Manchester or Barcelona pay for guided tours around Old Trafford or the Nou Camp. Lars found it just as exciting, just as exhilarating as they did, to stare at a plastic bench in a lino-covered dressing-room and think, 'So that's where Rudi Völler sits before each game.'

Reiner Calmund was sitting in the stadium restaurant when Rettig finally brought Lars in to see him. Bayer's general manager weighed in at about 24 stone, and his voluminous body was seen in the Bundesliga as a symbol of Calmund's power. He was a heavyweight in every respect. And when Calmund's belly advanced towards you, it was more than an abstract symbol of power, it was a real threat. You quickly felt backed into a corner. The general manager cheerfully stretched out a fleshy hand in greeting, and almost in the same breath he uttered a little introductory remark: 'I'll tell you quite honestly: at your age you don't actually become a professional. After all, you're going to be 27 in the summer. But Erich Ribbeck wants you, and here the coach gets what he wants. Our goalkeeping coach Werner Friese has watched you at Preussen a couple of times, and he's all for it as well, so what can I say? Can you imagine coming to play for us?'

Lars, don't put your foot in it now!

'Right now, I don't know, I've still got a job to do,' said Lars. **Damn, did that sound too stupid, too naive? But I really didn't know what Calmund was getting at: did he want me as a professional, or as a part-timer for the reserves?**

'Would I have to give up my job?'

'Of course you would, son. You're going to be training with the professionals.'

Professionals, he said professionals! OK. Stay cool.

'Yes, of course, the professionals. Then that's what I'd do.'

'Fine. Let's go to my office and see what we can do for you.'

I felt very hot. I had 50 yards from the restaurant to his office to work out what monthly wages I was going to ask for. Couldn't someone else do that for me?

In his office, Calmund walked around the desk, opened a drawer and pulled out two forms. Standard player contracts.

'So, what do we write in here?' Calmund said. 'OK, come on, let's do it differently. Let's turn it into a little game.'

'A game?'

'We take two pieces of paper, each of us writes down a sum, and then we see how far apart we are.'

I couldn't believe it. I couldn't believe it. I thought . . . I was sinking.

'Herr Calmund, I can't do that. I have absolutely no idea what a professional earns. If I write too much, you'll say, "What an arrogant arsehole you are." If I ask for too little, you'll laugh your head off. Either way, I'm going to end up losing.'

Calmund thought briefly. 'Fine, son. Let's do it this way: you get at least what I write down. Deal?'

Deal. Calmund handed Lars a little piece of paper and a biro.

What should I do now? Don't go too low: whatever he writes I am sure to have. But don't ask for too much, or he'll throw me out of his office.

Calmund wrote. Lars wrote.

'Finished?'

Lars nodded. Silently, almost conspiratorially, they switched pieces of paper. Calmund had written 12,000. Slowly, the goalkeeper looked up from the piece of paper into Calmund's eyes.

'Fine. Then we'll agree on 13,000 marks,' said the general manager.

'No, Herr Calmund, I wrote 14,000 marks [£4,500] and that's what I want. I've got a good job that I'm giving up, and a child to look after.'

For a moment I was shocked by myself. Are you round the bend, Lars, talking to him like that? But I quickly calmed down. He was prepared to haggle, he wanted to play. So he wouldn't be disturbed if I held out. Stay calm.

'OK 14,000 marks a month,' said Calmund. 'But then you'll only get 5,000 marks [£1,500] per game instead of the 6,000-mark appearance fee as you wrote.'

I was thinking: has Christmas come early?

'Fine.'

Calmund then wanted to know how long the contract should last.

'Three years plus the option of another season,' said Lars. He had read the bit about the option in a newspaper. Apparently many players insisted on it. He figured it was professional to put it in.

'Sorted,' said Calmund.

Five minutes and two signatures later, Lars was back outside. In just over six months' time, from 1 July 1996, he would be a professional, one of only 28 amateur footballers to receive a contract in the Bundesliga for the 1996/97 season. But none of the other 27 was as old as he was, and none of them had ever played so far down the table, in the Kreisliga. None of them had started his career at a pub-side tournament in the Westerwald.

Lars drove 200 yards away from the stadium, parked his

open-top Escort, switched off the engine and yelled, 'Yeeeeeeesssss! Yeeeeeeeesssss!' Then he continued driving, but he couldn't keep the news to himself for long. He stopped again, this time near a phone box. The first person he phoned was Daniela.

They were now a couple. Three days after Daniela had told him she wouldn't come and see him again, Lars had rung her up.

'It's all sorted out now,' he said.

'What is?'

'I've split up from my girlfriend. I'll come to your place at the weekend and we can talk about it.'

Normally people get to know each other, fall in love, have a child; in some cases something changes in their love, they become more like brother and sister, more best friends than a loving couple; and if they're unlucky they start fighting more often. Danny and I did everything the wrong way round. First of all we had a child, then we got to know each other, then we were the best of friends, then we said we'd stop seeing each other, and then we started to love each other. When she said she wasn't going to come to my place any more after Vivian's christening, I thought to myself, 'You're always talking about what a great woman Danny is, how well you get on, what a great mate she is. So, haven't you worked it out yet? She isn't a mate, this is love.' I realised that fully for the first time in December 1995. And immediately after that I got my professional contract in Leverkusen. It was really incredible. Since we'd been together, really together, all of a sudden everything was looking up. As though everything was growing through our love.

Anticipation of a professional life didn't alter the fact that Lars still had to wait six months for it. He knew he would soon be earning 14,000 marks a month, but until then he couldn't afford a thing, because he was still carrying his debts from his time with Wissen around with him. He knew he would soon be training with internationals, but for the moment he was still mooching around in an ashpit with Preussen Cologne. And all of a sudden no one was saying 'Wow, cool!' when he went up for a cross. Instead they said, 'Yeah, fine, and he's got a professional contract with Leverkusen as well.'

Winfried Pütz was furious that Lars had signed a contract with Leverkusen without telling him anything about it. He, the Preussen chairman, had assured Dortmund that his goalkeeper would drop by again in the spring. Lars himself was cross that Pütz was arranging a friendly during the winter break – against Bayer Leverkusen. 'Are you trying to make me look ridiculous?' Lars moaned. 'What am I going to look like if I let a goal in? Then I turn up in Leverkusen next summer and the team'll be saying, "Oh, yeah, remember? We knocked six goals past him last time he played. He's a lemon."'

The day before the match he had got himself so terrified about dropping the ball that he couldn't sleep.

Preussen lost the friendly 3–0. It was a good result for everyone. On a bitterly cold evening, and with his nerves on end, Lars had even saved a penalty taken by world champion Rudi Völler, and then heard a few choice words from Leverkusen's coach Erich Ribbeck. Rüdiger Vollborn, Leverkusen's substitute goalkeeper, was already 34, and Lars would have a real chance to take Vollborn's place on the subs' bench, said Ribbeck. He then offered Lars an early start: although he was contracted to play for Preussen until June, he was welcome to train in Leverkusen from 1 April.

Actually, as far as Lars Leese was concerned, it all began on 31 March. In his mind's eye he worked out the way his first day as a professional footballer would go. He was already greeting Rudi Völler. 'Great to meet you, Rudi, we played against each other one time' – 'Oh, yeah, you're the guy who saved my penalty in that friendly.' He was already diving full stretch to tip a bullet from Ulf Kirsten around the post. The goalkeeping coach Werner Friese was already whispering to him, 'Son, Vollborn's going to have to stretch himself to claim his place as second goalkeeper.' And in the dressing-room he was being welcomed with a grunt by the kitman: 'What have we here, another new boy? More kit for me to wash?' Actually, Lars wasn't imagining that one. That was what really happened when he turned up at the Bayer ground. Welcome to the world of professional football.

When you dream of life as a professional footballer, you see yourself with just the keeper to beat, the ball rocketing into the top-left corner, the net snapping back with the force of your shot. You see the terraces behind the goal with a thousand outstretched hands in the air, just the hands; the rest of the spectators' bodies are just pale dots as far as you're concerned. You see the other players piling on top of you in celebration, and the photograph in the paper with you right at the bottom of a happy mountain of people, your smiling face poking out between hairy legs and football boots. You see yourself being interviewed, journalists jostling, fans yelling from the third row.

What Lars Leese saw was that even the dream profession has its trainees. He was right in the midst of it, yet he wasn't really part of it. He trained with the other two goalkeepers, Dirk Heinen and Rüdiger Vollborn, but he didn't see himself as their equal. More of a fan than anything. 'I've never seen jumping power like Heinen's before. He and I are worlds apart,' he told Daniela at home. But he was still dreamy enough not to be disturbed by such discoveries.

Daniel Ischdonat was still there, although in July he would leave the post of third goalkeeper to Lars and transfer to Regionalliga side Eintracht Trier. After a few days he asked Lars what he hoped for from his time in Leverkusen. 'To be first sub for Heinen,' Lars replied. 'Vollborn is a nut I can crack.'

The next day, Vollborn came into the dressing-room with a face like ten wet Wednesdays. Werner Friese, the goal-keeping coach, beckoned Lars over with raised eyebrows and a surly nod of the head, and tore into him.

'What the hell do you think you're playing at? You've only been here a few days and already you're causing trouble.'

'What?'

'Telling Ischdonat you'd get Vollborn out of the way. You can stop that crap for starters, we don't play that kind of politics around here.'

I was flabbergasted. First that Ischdonat would have passed on what I said to Vollborn. 'You should have expected that, they've been training together for two years,' Friese said to me. He was probably right. But I'd have expected a different reaction from Vollborn. He had 400 Bundesliga games under his belt, he'd won the UEFA Cup; in his place I'd have gone over to me and said, 'Listen, mate, you play a few Bundesliga games and when you've done that get back to me.' Instead he gets all huffy and complains to the coach. We trained side by side in silence for a few days before I went up to him. 'So what do you want from me, Rüdiger? Do you want me to see you as a footballing god, you want me to be glad I'm alive, not to dare go anywhere near you? We all want to be the best. You've got to allow me a little ambition.' Then everything was OK. Rüdiger's the kind of guy who can't really stay angry with anyone. But I was left with the fact that something trivial like that can turn into a huge fuss in a professional team.

Could it be that I've been wrong about Leese? the goalkeeping coach wondered a little later. From what Werner Friese had seen, it wasn't like him. Friese put the friction with Vollborn down to the new boy's naivety. The boy wasn't malicious, but was he good enough? Four times he'd watched him playing with Preussen, and he'd been struck by the extraordinary speed of his reactions. Friese had also been impressed by the way Lars organised his defence, almost like a great conductor. But now that he had him there every day, he suddenly saw what shortcomings Lars possessed, too. He might be nearly six and a half feet tall, but loads of high balls got past him, and for crosses he hardly left the ground. Did he have no jumping power in his legs at all? 'What sort of a guy have you got there?' Rudi Völler asked the goalkeeping coach. Friese's heart pounded.

Friese had spent the early part of his career playing in goal in Dresden, and had come to West Germany after the wall came down. By 1996, after only two years in Leverkusen, he was seen as the best goalkeeping coach in Germany. But his reputation wasn't so secure that he could laugh off criticism. He lived in constant fear that a goalkeeper he had recommended would be unmasked as a lemon.

He gave Lars extra coaching, and plenty of it.

Throughout this time there were two Lars Leeses. One of them played on Saturday with Preussen Cologne in the Oberliga, entirely at ease, often playing extremely well, apparently at the height of his powers: the other drove every morning from Monday to Friday to Leverkusen and began, at the age of 27, to study the rudiments of goalkeeping for the first time in his life. He swapped these identities as though it was the most natural thing in the world: on Saturday he was the champion, during the week the apprentice. At Leverkusen he threw himself at the strikers' feet, just as he had been doing for years in amateur football, and saw with surprise that they didn't just shoot, they waited until he was on the ground then casually lobbed it over him or dribbled around him. They called it 'goalie-watching'.

In the Kreisliga the strikers just shut their eyes and kick. It's all predictable: he draws back, and just before he kicks the ball you can tell from his posture which way it's going to go. So you just jump accordingly. If you do that in the Bundesliga you just fly into the void. They can change their shooting position and thus the direction of the ball in a split second. If you go too early – say, the moment their shooting leg swings back you head for the left corner – then they say thanks, feint, and put the ball to your right. And you're left lying there like an idiot. I had to learn not to react too quickly to the attacker's body language, and then, when they shot, to move much faster. It's a matter of tiny fractions of a second, and at first, when you haven't yet got it instinctively and one of them shows up in front of your goal, you say to yourself, 'Stand there, don't lie down too quickly like you did last time!' But you can't actually think the thought all the way through: your radar's already roaring at you: 'Now! Jump!' And then the ball comes at you even harder. The force of it really throws your hands back.

Even when he made the switch from the Kreisliga to the Oberliga, it had taken Lars six months to find his feet at that higher level. Presumably this was much the same. Or perhaps not. Was he reaching his limit? One thought he kept to himself: 'Man, you're never going to make it.' Goalkeepers are always vacillating between extreme confidence and existential anxiety, because they know their luck can do a 180-degree turn over nothing. A tiny blunder can lead to a goal.

Friese taught Lars to keep his hands straight when he was catching, not to bend them back. A hundred times he told him to move a yard and a half forwards when Lars was standing too close to the goal-line – a classic reflex on the part of goalkeepers when they get frightened: they pull back as far as possible. Friese sent him over hurdles for hours, and to the gym to develop his jumping power. 'You're like a sculptor chiselling away at the perfect goalkeeper: a bit here, a bit there,' Lars told Friese. He called him 'da Vinci'.

These were bad times for trainees with Bayer. Coach and players weren't overly concerned about whether the new third goalkeeper was going to cope. The club he was joining was on the way to relegation to the Zweite Bundesliga with one of the best and most expensive teams in the country. Before the winter break, Bayer Leverkusen had been one of the leading teams in the Bundesliga. But when the 1995/96 season resumed, things had gone badly wrong, very quickly. As so often happens when first-class teams suddenly take a tumble, Bayer was more or less helpless in the face of these unfamiliar difficulties. Erich Ribbeck simply ignored the crisis. When he announced at the end of April, 'I think it would be madness to put the players under even more pressure by talking about the UEFA Cup,' general manager Calmund had to remind the coach that no one was talking about qualification for the UEFA Cup any more and that

Ribbeck should set his sights a little further down the table. Ribbeck, who enjoyed the easy life just as much as he liked endless sentences full of interlocking clauses that generally led nowhere, couldn't work up any enthusiasm – and, more to the point, couldn't enthuse his team – for the tedious scramble to stay in the top division. He often got his assistant Peter Hermann to organise training. He would watch for the first half hour, but when the players came back from the pitch after 90 minutes, they would be lucky to catch a glimpse of him.

Ribbeck never shook off the damage that his image suffered during this time. He had been a successful coach in the seventies and eighties, but he was to be a complete write-off as national coach in the 2000 European Championship. Not even his own team could take him seriously. The symbol of this was supplied by Germany's goalkeeper Oliver Kahn at a Euro 2000 press conference he attended with Ribbeck. While the coach was talking, Kahn pointedly flicked through a sports magazine; he didn't even stop when Wolfgang Niersbach, the press officer, nudged him with his elbow. The German team was knocked out in the early stages.

Back at Leverkusen in 1996, Ribbeck was fired four weeks before the end of the season, but when the season's last day arrived Bayer were still in danger of going down. A draw in the last game against Kaiserslautern would be enough, but Kaiserslautern were also battling to stay up. It was set to be a huge game. One of the two clubs was going to be relegated.

It was an especially tense time for Lars: he had become aware some time before that his contract wasn't valid for the Zweite Bundesliga.

**That was what I got out of being such a gambler,
out of going to Calmund without an agent. What a
beginner's mistake that was, only signing a contract
for the Erste Bundesliga. And now Ribbeck, the coach
who thought highly of me and wanted to make me
a rival to Vollborn, had been fired. I couldn't just go
up to the manager and say, 'Hey, Calli, just add in a
bit about the Zweite Bundesliga, OK?' I would have
been thrown on the scrap-heap as a pessimist. What,
you think we're going to go down? They'd have
thrown me out on the spot. We've no use for nega-
tive-thinking people like that! Please God, I thought,
just let them win on Saturday.**

Lars stood with Daniela and her father outside the stadium
and watched the team bus drive by. Behind the tinted glass
the Leverkusen players looked like zombies. Perhaps it was
just his imagination – but then how would you expect players to look on a day like that?

Pavel Kuka's goal for Kaiserslautern in the 58th minute
was a long time coming. It was desperation that had driven
them on from the first minute, despair that had paralysed
the Leverkusen players.

**It was all over now. I sat there on the stupid grand-
stand and impotently watched us going down. We
were going down. A new coach would come and say,
'Thanks, Mr Leese, I don't need you.' For six months
I'd been hearing everyone say, 'That's fantastic, you're
going to be a professional.' For three months I'd been
training here along with everyone else, and now it
was all over. Now I was unemployed.**

If the worst comes to the worst, next year you can always play Bezirksliga again, I said to myself. Who else is going to take me? The clubs have already decided their recruitment plans for next season, even in the Regionalliga.

At least one member of the Leverkusen squad was playing outstandingly well, but as the goalkeeper Dirk Heinen was only able to prevent things getting even worse. No saviour was in sight. The crowd was yelling with excitement; there were 6,000 Kaiserslautern fans in the stadium. For Rudi Völler, the old battle-horse, it would be his last Bundesliga game whatever happened. Now aged 36, and at the end of his career, Völler was no longer capable of magic, but he still knew every trick in the book. Once again he managed to wangle himself a free-kick, 30 yards from the goal. The Kaiserslautern players protested, but they were too late. Völler had already taken it, passing to Mike Rietpitsch, who shot from 25 yards out, hard but at a comfortable height. Lars knew any decent amateur keeper would have saved it. But Andreas Reinke, Kaiserslautern's goalkeeper, couldn't hold on and the ball bounced back into the middle of the penalty area. Markus Münch belted the rebound into the net, bringing the score to 1–1. Nine minutes before the end of the Bundesliga season.

Oooooaaaaahhhh! That was all I felt: oooooaaaah-hhh! Relief. Happiness. Maybe I should not have been worried about my contract. Maybe in retrospect they would have given me one for the Zweite Bundesliga, presumably for less money. I don't know, I never asked. And I don't want to know.

Three days later, Bayer Leverkusen went on an end-of-season tour to the USA and Mexico. It wasn't the same team Lars had spent two months training with. This one could afford to laugh.

For the first time he had the feeling that this really was the dream, the way you imagine being a professional footballer when you're playing in tiny places like Neitersen or Guckheim. He had played his last game for Preussen Cologne in front of 400 spectators in Solingen, and now he was keeping himself warm as substitute goalkeeper in a friendly against the Mexican champions America in front of a packed stadium of 80,000. He felt like a singer with the Backstreet Boys. Every time he did his stretching exercises on the touchline a great cry went up from thousands of young spectators. The only player on the Leverkusen team the Mexican crowd knew was Rudi Völler. Before the game, one of his last for the club, he'd been presented with a bunch of flowers to honour his achievements during a long career. But the young fans treated the rest of the German players as stars as well, just to keep things simple. They particularly liked cheering on the tall, blond substitute keeper. Even if the coach only let him warm up.

Lars was in a good mood when he got back to the dressing-room after the game. He stood under the shower and thought to himself, 'Wasn't there something else?' Then he remembered. 'Rudi!' he shouted, and Völler, the superstar with a crown of suds on his head, turned round. In all seriousness, Lars Leese, who had saved every single newspaper cutting from his amateur days, said to Rudi Völler, who must have forgotten more headlines than Lars could ever hope to receive, 'You left your flowers on the subs' bench, Rudi.'

4

THE THIRD-CHOICE
BUNDESLIGA KEEPER

LARS FOUND THE first signs of fame in his pigeonhole at
the start of the 1996/97 season: autograph cards. A
picture of himself, 3,000 times, in the green Bayer shirt. The
cards had to be returned to the office, signed, within four
days so that the club could send them out.

He called Daniela from the car. The box of 3,000 Lars
Leeses was on the passenger seat. 'I've got autograph cards
– is that fantastic or what?' he said. 'I'll be home in a minute.'

And then he started writing. He wrote *Lars Leese* in a
black art pen, very carefully, very formally. After 30 minutes
he was writing only *L. Leese*, after an hour *Leese*, and later
just *Lee*— with a long tail that could, with a little effort, be
interpreted as *se*. He spent two evenings at the sitting-room
table. Now and then he would curse.

'What's up?' asked Daniela.

'I've just automatically written *L. Leese* again. Because of
that damned *L* I'll probably still be sitting here for another
two hours, but it just keeps slipping out.'

Things had changed since his beginners' course in April and May: he now felt like a real professional. It was true that the new head-coach, Christoph Daum, had left the old pecking-order among the goalkeepers intact, so that as third-choice goalkeeper Lars wouldn't even have a seat on the subs' bench. For the time being he would only be playing in Bayer's reserve team in the North Rhine Oberliga, the same division he had played in with Preussen Cologne. But he didn't need to be playing in the Bundesliga to feel like a professional. For the time being it was enough to be around for training and playing the fool – to be accepted as an equal by his colleagues. Since their trip to Mexico he had felt he was one of them. He might have been the least important part, but he *was* a part of the team. The other players liked his cheerfulness; perhaps unconsciously they liked him all the more because he was only the third-choice goalkeeper, which meant that he wasn't a real threat to anyone. True, he wasn't allowed to play, but he could still insult the coach's wife with impunity.

'Come on Uschi, you old tart!' he called out happily in the Cologne restaurant Maca Ronni, three sheets to the wind, cigar in hand, to Christoph Daum's wife, and gave her a beaming smile. Daum had invited the team and all the backroom staff along with their wives to the restaurant to celebrate his appointment. During the preparations for the season, Daum had warned the players time and again that a wild night on the town would wipe out two days of training, but now, for one evening, he was ignoring his own advice. They drank whatever was on the drinks menu. Because the atmosphere was so relaxed, Uschi Daum was able to laugh at Lars' crude joke. Standing next to him, his girlfriend Daniela wanted to sink into the floor, but he couldn't understand what was so embarrassing about his behaviour. 'So many people are serious, tense, awkwardly polite when they're talking to a famous footballer or his wife,' he told Daniela, 'but these guys just want to have a bit of fun. They want you to act completely normal.' Daniela still wasn't entirely sure if it was normal to call the coach's wife an old tart with a wide smile on your face.

Immediately after the party, at four o'clock in the morning, her boyfriend demonstrated another example of how he talked to famous footballers, now that they were his colleagues. They climbed into his car in the car park, but when they tried to set off the car just hopped forwards. There was a puncture in one of the front tyres. Someone had knifed it.

Lars had got the open-top Golf on special terms from a dealer in Leverkusen. In return, the dealer had placed stickers saying RHENUS CAR SHOWROOM SPONSORS THE FOOT-BALLERS OF BAYER 04 on the doors. The stickers must have driven the Cologne supporters wild, Lars was sure. After all, he had been one of them himself for long enough. And now he was playing for Bayer, their arch-rivals.

'Stop! Everybody stop!' he shouted. Daniela beeped the horn. Ulf Kirsten and Hans-Peter Lehnhoff, two Bayer players who had gone with Lars to the multi-storey, came to a halt in their cars. 'Someone's punctured my tyres.'

Faster than Lars could take it in, Lehnhoff arrived with an enormous toolbox. Kristen was already furiously jacking up the car. At four o'clock in the morning in a Cologne multi-storey car park, two of the best-known footballers in Germany worked away on Lars' car in their designer suits. He stood next to them, shouting, 'Faster, faster! Let's make this a Formula One pitstop. I'll stop the clock!'

'For Christ's sake, would you just shut the fuck up?' Kirsten complained. But even he had to laugh.

Freed from the stress of playing on Saturdays, Lars greed-ily absorbed all the little moments that made up the world of professional football. Frantisek Straka, his team-mate from Preussen, who had played Bundesliga football in a Borussia Mönchengladbach and a Hansa Rostock shirt, had advised him, 'You look around, it's a shark tank. Twenty-five guys fighting mercilessly from Monday to Friday for the 11 places on Saturday.' Lars soon knew what Straka meant. Ulf Kirsten and Christian Wörns, for example, Bayer's outstanding play-ers, were forever winding each other up during training. They kicked, shoved and insulted each other, and hardly anyone would have been so deluded as to think that their fouls on each other were accidental. They were fighting for the leading role in the team. Primeval rituals of masculin-ity still have their part to play in modern football. But the internal competition wasn't entirely unscrupulous. A profes-sional squad is a shark tank with social rules. When a bunch of players sat down for salad and pasta in the Taxi Pizza restaurant at lunchtime between training sessions, or with the whole team in the VIP lounge after a home game, Lars felt right at home. The camaraderie, the banter – it was no different from the Kreisliga. Except that the food was better.

Years later, when he was in England and speaking to old colleagues from Leverkusen on the phone, they complained that the atmosphere had never again been as good as it had been in 1996/97. But was that really a surprise? They'd never played as well again as they had that season. After nine games without a defeat and five crucial goals from Ulf Kirsten, the team was going places. Kirsten had made the difference; all his team-mates thought Ulf was 'a bit of a star'.

Leverkusen had pulled back from the brink of relegation to become a candidate for the championship. At a time when sports journalism in Germany had decided that the real battlefield was not on the pitch, but in the players' psyches, Bayer Leverkusen and their head-coach Christoph Daum became the case study of the season. Daum, who at press conferences would open his eyes wide and talk about the seething fire in the team that had to become a raging blaze, had already supplied Freudian-minded football journalists with plenty of copy when he was coaching FC Cologne and VfB Stuttgart. He would continue to do so into the new millennium until, in autumn 2000, he was suspended for snorting cocaine. No profile of him could neglect to mention that he had laid out 30,000 marks (some £10,000) in cash – the sum each player would get if they won the champion-ship – in the dressing-room before a match in Stuttgart, and that at Leverkusen he'd made the players run over broken glass. The German tabloid *Bild* called him 'the motivator', and the *Frankfurter Rundschau* reckoned 'he could sell fridges to Eskimos'. Having grown up in a working-class housing estate in Duisburg, all of a sudden he was greatly in demand with major companies at seminars on personnel manage-ment. There, Daum informed them, 'You'll get closest to your people in the shower.' The crowd watched in fasci-nation as Daum switched from hard-headed prole, hurling insults at studio host Jupp Heynckes on the ZDF television programme *Sportstudio*, to consummate politician, comment-ing on Leverkusen's exit from the European Cup with a statesmanlike 'Something is wrong in the National League.' He analysed his television interviews afterwards on video just as he analysed his team's games.

During these public performances, he was in fact satisfy-ing his need for attention rather than motivating his players. As Daum himself said in the dressing-room, 'If you watch TV tomorrow, you needn't believe what I say. I've got myself out of another hole, I know what the point of it was. But you can ignore all that. You should only pay attention to what I say in here.'

Christoph Daum was everything that Erich Ribbeck wasn't: fanatical and strong-willed. His motto was always: 'Justify your existence. Every day you've got to justify the fact that you have a job that millions dream of.' And you believed him. Not because he said things like that, but because he lived them out. Even while he was coaching, Ribbeck was on his way to the golf course; Daum's light was still on in his office at nine o'clock at night. For example, before we played against HSV he discovered on video that the Hamburg team always left a gap in the middle of the penalty area during corners. It was only about a yard across, but he'd seen it. So the week before the match he had us practise that for hours: corners delivered right into the unmarked spot, a player shooting into the gap, and bang, there you are. On Saturday against Hamburg we scored two goals like that. It was always that way. When we were up against Freiburg, he said, 'Low through-balls from the wings into the six-yard box – that'll give them problems.' For a week we did nothing else in training but that. The goalkeepers were going around the bend because the balls were constantly being fired in around our ears, but on Saturday we scored a goal that way. He had a brilliant eye for detail, and he was ruthless in his attempts to achieve perfection. Once, when the team came home at three in the morning after a European Cup match, he switched on the floodlights and sent the squad out to run about. At three in the morning. As far as I was concerned he wasn't just a great motivator, as the papers were always saying, he was a real football man, totally obsessed. He knew everything there was to know. When it came out that he was taking cocaine, I was just as surprised as any of his fans. I would never have guessed that Daum was on drugs. When people say now that the players had known about it for ages, it's nonsense. No one had the slightest notion. On the other hand, I haven't the faintest idea how you can tell if someone's coked up. He doesn't stagger around the place like a drunk. Of course it was obvious that a club committed to the anti-drug campaign would have to fire him. Personally, as a player, I wouldn't have a problem with being coached by a coke-head. If he works as well, and with such commitment, as Daum did at Leverkusen, I couldn't care less what he puts up his nose when he's not working.

Lars watched from the grandstand with the rest of the reserve players as Bayer, under Daum, rapidly established itself as Bayern Munich's fiercest rivals in the Bundesliga. Daniela, by now Frau Leese, watched from the directors' box.

A footballer's wife effectively marries into the game, and this means that she has her own part to play in the spectacle of professional football. Shelley Webb, herself married to Neil Webb, the former Nottingham Forest, Manchester United and England player, described the role in these terms: 'Football is God. The men live for it, and their wives are just another piece of kit – like their shinpads.'

Leverkusen was a club that put great amounts of energy into finding the perfect working conditions for professional footballers, into trying to get the details exactly right. Bayer took care of everything, from shinpads to the players' wives.

They were invited into the VIP areas and given seats in the directors' box. As they all sat there side by side they looked like a team in their own right, and that was how they behaved as well: the competition in Wives United was just as fierce as it was among the husbands. Who had the best outfit? Who was wearing the most hairspray? 'So, before the game one of them would say, "Look at this watch, my husband gave it to me," and come the next match you could bet that someone else would be wearing exactly the same watch. Only with an extra jewel on it,' said Daniela. Sometimes she was amazed that 'the footballers, who were seen as gods, all turned out to be nice and normal, while their wives behaved like divas'. But in Sandra Heinen and Susi Lehnhoff she found two like-minded friends, and by and large she had a great time in Wives United. There was all the bitching, for a start. And all the places you fetched up – even in 'real pimps' discos'. While their husbands were off at training camp, the wives staged their own competitive evenings (charades rather than football), organised, appropriately enough, by Uschi Daum, the coach's wife. Daniela got on well with Uschi, although she shouldn't have: how dare the wife of the third-choice goalkeeper be friends with the coach's wife? There was no question of envy, said Daniela – she had her ways of dealing with that. Once, in the VIP lounge, just as Christian Wörns' wife was telling everyone how much her blouse had cost, a spoonful of tiramisu landed with a splat on the exquisite material. Daniela happened to be standing right opposite her, but she thinks she managed to make the whole thing look like an accident.

The husbands' lives, in contrast, were really boring. Lars had been aware that Bayer Leverkusen wasn't going to be Real Madrid, with screaming, bra-throwing teenagers at the training ground. But it was still startling that the club's hard-core fan base consisted of two girls whom no one in their right mind would have entered in a beauty contest. Ninety-five per cent of Bundesliga professionals, he observed, only encountered anything like mass worship on Saturday after-noon in the stadium. Ten of them could walk through Leverkusen at lunchtime, and unless Ulf Kirsten was among them no one would stop them for an autograph. At home in Hürth, his old friends from BC Efferen asked him eagerly for the latest stories from the world of the stars, but he had to admit that on their most recent outing the entire team had gone to a posh club called Halle Eins. They'd left three hours later, practically unrecognised.

By the end of the 96/97 pre-season, after months of being drilled by Werner Friese, Lars had visibly changed. The daily special training, the endless jumping of hurdles and the weightlifting in the gym had turned him into a real athlete. His weight had risen from $13\frac{1}{2}$ stone to $14\frac{1}{2}$ stone. During winter training in a camp in Orlando, Rudi Völler, who'd become head of sport at Bayer after the end of his foot-balling career, asked Friese, 'What have you done to him?' Even Friese, who was terrified of criticism and for that reason was quick to sniff it out everywhere, understood that Völler's question could only be a compliment. 'Lars was in such good form that Dirk Heinen and Rüdiger Vollborn were completely gobsmacked,' says Friese. 'He was on the way to becoming real competition for them.'

Lars himself felt that he was becoming a better goal-keeper. But on the pitch he seemed to be getting worse. As a professional on the Leverkusen reserve team playing in the Oberliga, he wasn't as consistently good as he had been when playing as an amateur with Preussen Cologne in the same league. He was now jumping more powerfully and his positional play was more confident, but he was still letting in goals he was sure he would have saved the previous year.

It was like a child who attracts attention in school as this fantastic tennis player, so he gets sent to a club. There, the coach tells the boy for the first time that he does indeed have a massive gift, but he's twisting his shoulder too much on his returns, his arm's bending too much on his forehands, and on his serves he nearly keels over. Each time he hits the ball the boy can only think about his shoulder, his arm, his body, and not about where he's supposed to be hitting the ball. I'd just been following my instincts for 20 years. If I threw myself at the ball I had never thought about how I was jumping or how I was holding my hands. And all of a sudden I was thinking, 'Keep your hands straight when you're catching, Lars. What did Friese tell you? Another five feet forwards.' I was like the boy who is just as preoccupied with himself as he is with the game.

Shortly before Christmas Tony Woodcock, Lars' old coach at Preussen, called him. Woodcock had come as a player to FC Cologne from Nottingham Forest in the eighties. Apart from Kevin Keegan, he was the only British footballer who had ever managed to gain acceptance in the Bundesliga. Fifteen years later he was still in the Rhineland, working as a pundit on British football for German television and as an adviser to British clubs about German players. He told Lars he had something for him. Viv Anderson, the coach of English Premier League club Middlesbrough, was looking for a goalkeeper.

Clubs send their scouts all over the world, keep detailed files on potential recruits, but when it comes down to it, managers often just try out whoever they fancy. There might not be a scouting report, the manager might not even have seen the player himself – a quiet word from a friend can be recommendation enough. And that's what happened here. Viv Anderson is a good friend of Tony Woodcock, Tony Woodcock used to be Lars Leese's coach, so Lars Leese, Leverkusen's third-choice goalkeeper, went for a trial at Middlesbrough.

Daniela bought a travel-guide to England to find out where she might be living in the future, but when her husband came back from the north-east he couldn't tell her whether the book would be any use to her or not. After his three-day trial, no one in Middlesbrough had told Lars what they thought of him. Thanks very much for coming, they'd let Woodcock know – that was all Anderson told him when he sent him on his way. Players normally know least about what's going on, particularly when it comes to the issue of whether a club wants to buy or sell them, and most of them put up with it in silence. They put their future into the hands of agents or advisers and wait in quiet uncertainty to see what happens.

Two days later, Woodcock called Lars. Middlesbrough wanted him, straight away. Lars was to ask Bayer Leverkusen if they would release him.

That's how things are in football: the chances come out of nowhere, and at random. You don't have much time to think – are you going to like it there, will your wife be OK, what's the food going to be like? – you just have to pack your bags and go. With Middlesbrough I'd earn twice as much money, and

all of a sudden I might get to be number one. So next morning I knocked on Christoph Daum's door. He didn't even think for a second: no, under no circumstances would he let me go now, in the middle of the season. He didn't have three goalkeepers just for fun, he would need me if one of the other two was injured. Anyone else would have slammed the door with rage when they left Daum's office, but I wanted to stick both arms in the air in celebration and shout 'Yeah!' I was that happy. For the first time I had felt how valuable I was to the coach and the club, and at that moment I thought that was better than any transfer in the world.

Now, after receiving this fillip from Daum, Lars wanted more: the chance to sit, just once, on the subs' bench.

After their initial skirmish, Lars had got on very well with Rüdiger Vollborn. But that didn't change the fact that Vollborn was clinging on to the subs' bench with all his might. The Freudian sports journalists of the nineties identified sitting on the subs' bench as the most severe professional illness in football, the greatest imaginable punishment for a sportsman — being forced to be a passive spectator. Pictures of highly paid, sad-eyed stars watching their colleagues at work on the pitch made the back pages just as often as pictures of the game itself. If you bear in mind that a professional club employs between 25 and 32 players, and only 11 or (with substitutions) at the most 14 can play, it becomes clear that for almost half of all professional footballers the subs' bench is actually a viable goal. Financially, too: in the 1996/97 season Leverkusen paid each of their players a 9,000-mark (about £3,000) bonus for every game, they won. The men on the subs' bench got 50 per cent of that, and the ones in the stand got nothing. Vollborn had played 397 Bundesliga games and only two years earlier had had to watch Dirk Heinen oust him from the goal. He didn't want to be toppled from the subs' bench at the age of 34 on top of everything else.

When Bayer played indoor football during winter-break exhibitions, Daum saw them simply as spectacles and left it up to his goalkeepers to sort out their own line-ups. Heinen said he didn't want to play indoors at all. Vollborn said in that case he would play all the matches.

'Couldn't you let me on for ten minutes? At least I'd feel I'd been there,' Lars pleaded at their last tournament in Berlin.

'Look, I'm really sorry, but Berlin's my home town, and I want to be the best goalkeeper in the tournament while we're here,' said Vollborn.

By that point Lars knew that it would be a matter of luck for him to end up on the subs' bench – bad luck for Vollborn, that is. Lars would simply have to wait for his rival to be injured. There aren't many professions in which you work closely with your colleagues, support them, encourage them, perhaps even understand them better than anyone else, while waiting patiently for some misfortune to befall them. A couple of times that season Vollborn picked up minor injuries early in the week, and on the Thursday goalkeeping coach Friese would say to Lars, 'Bring your club kit with you tomorrow. We don't know what sort of a state Rüdiger's going to be in, and you might have to sit on the bench on Saturday.' But when he got to the dressing-room on the Friday for the last training sension before the match, Vollborn's kit would already be on the hook. The dark-blue jacket yelled in Lars' face: 'I, Rüdiger Vollborn, am not going to give up my place on the subs' bench, even if I'm carrying my head under my arm.'

Despite the knockback, Viv Anderson had not forgotten the lanky German goalkeeper. Anderson no longer needed Lars – by now Middlesbrough had filled the position with Australian Mark Schwarzer of FC Kaiserslautern – but he did recommend Lars to another club. Danny Wilson, the manager of Barnsley, called Tony Woodcock. He was looking for a goalkeeper for the coming season, and he wanted to know whether that tall guy who had been to Middlesbrough might be able to come to him for a trial. Woodcock passed on the request, telling Lars, 'It's not a pretty town and the club's only in the First Division.' But at the time Barnsley were doing well there was a good chance that they'd be in the Premiership for the 1997/98 season, and as for the town itself, well, he certainly wouldn't be making bad money. If he could stay with Bayer Leverkusen until the end of the 1996/97 season, and if the English team were willing to pay a decent transfer fee, then this time the club might be able to let him go, Christoph Daum said in Leverkusen.

One Monday evening in March 1997, Lars flew to Manchester. Barnsley's team masseur formed the one-man welcoming committee. He chauffeured the German to South Yorkshire, and as they travelled along the A68 they soon saw the gentle green hills of the northern Peak District. In the past it had been a mining area; now it was a centre for leisure activities. Lars saw nothing of the town of Barnsley, for trials are usually rather miserable affairs. Twenty-year-old boys come from countries like Ghana and Finland to small towns in Britain or Belgium and they're dumped in four-star hotels on the edge of town where they hang around forlornly in their rooms or else stroll aimlessly through the hotel gardens. They don't explore the town, they have to save themselves for their trials. Lars zapped through the TV channels in his room in the Ardsley House Hotel. There were only four of them. He switched the TV off and lay about on the bed.

On Tuesday morning, he went for training in Barnsley. Once they got started, all he could make out was the word 'fuckin''. Fuckin' this, fuckin' that. What exactly 'fuckin'', was he didn't know because of the strong accents of most of the players. He just thought they must be pretty full on. Later, when he lived in England, he discovered that the word 'fuckin'', in the language of English footballers, just gives a bit of an extra edge to what they're saying. And after a while he came to quite like it. 'Fuckin' play the fuckin' ball, for fuck's sake!'

The way in which the players expressed themselves wasn't the only thing that struck him the first time he went for training in Barnsley. There was also, for example, the training ground. He'd been expecting something like a soft English lawn, but there was hardly anything there that looked even remotely green. Barnsley had only two training pitches, and after eight months of a season during which the first, reserve and youth teams had ploughed up the grass with their studded boots there was practically nothing left of the pitch but sand and soil. And then there was the manager, Danny Wilson, who had brought him in for his trial – he didn't even turn up. The first team was playing that evening. Only the reserves were training.

I found myself wondering what on earth was going on. The manager had brought me from Germany specially, and now he didn't even want to see me play? I was disappointed. That evening I watched the Barnsley game, or at least what could be seen of it: the fog was so thick that you couldn't see as far as the other side of the pitch. It was slowly starting to seem a bit weird. Where on earth had I ended up?

There were another two training days planned with Barnsley, and the next morning, once again, only the reserve team was there. But at least the manager turned up this time. When he said hello I could tell he was impressed by the size of me. Wilson stared at me and beamed, 'You're tall!' During training, one of those things we in Germany call a 'moon ball' came into my penalty area – a mishit cross that hangs in the air for ages before dropping almost vertically out of the sky. It's a thankless task for goalkeepers, because the strikers are lurking behind you like vultures, pushing and shoving, and you have all that time on your hands to think, 'Oh Christ, what if I drop the ball?' When I jumped, I pushed the strikers away with my shoulders, caught the ball and, as I came back down again, the strikers were on the ground on either side of me. Wilson yelled, 'Hey, you're my man!' I thought, 'Hmm, what's happened now?' But in the three days I was there that was the only moment I got any feedback at all. On the Thursday I finally got to train with the first team, but we only did an easy 45 minutes because they were playing again on the Saturday. I returned home and thought, 'Fantastic, you were there for three days and they can't even organise a proper training session so that you can show what you're capable of.'

'How was it?' Woodcock asked him when he got back. 'I have no idea, Tony,' said Lars.

'No problem,' said Woodcock. It's his favourite phrase: no problem. At some point very early on in life, Woodcock had noticed that a casual air and a permanent smile will get you a long way. No problem, he would ring Danny Wilson.

In mid-April he was on the phone again.

'No problem, Lars, they want you.'

'I'm sorry?'

'Yeah, it's fine. You'll be on £120,000 a year.'

'But Tony, we haven't even discussed money.'

'Yeah, fine, no problem. The money's all sorted. We'll fly out on Wednesday and you'll see.'

Lars didn't have much thinking to do; he had already done his thinking in December when he had gone to Middlesbrough. If he got the chance, he would move to England. There was no way of telling whether he would make much more headway in Leverkusen – perhaps he'd be able to nudge his way in front of Vollborn, but there was no chance anyone was going to get past Heinen, who was being talked of as an international goalkeeper after an excellent season. Daniela had told Lars she would travel anywhere.

Late in the morning of 23 April 1997, he arrived at Oakwell with Woodcock. Danny Wilson and the club chairman John Dennis, a wholesale greengrocer, were waiting for them. 'One more thing,' Woodcock had said in the hire car. 'I've told them that you're second-choice goalkeeper at Leverkusen, not third. OK? Apart from that, let me do the talking.'

But not much talking was done. Wilson and Woodcock had already sorted out the financial side of things on the phone. Lars would get a one-off payment of £18,000 at the start of each season, and then £2,000 a week. Traditionally, businesses in Great Britain paid wages weekly, and not usually by bank transfer, as they did in Germany, but with a cheque. Every Friday, footballers emerged from offices all over England with a little brown envelope – a touching anachronism in an age when these unremarkable recycled envelopes could contain cheques to the tune of £10,000 or more. At

Leverkusen, Lars had been earning 168,000 marks a year, or just over £55,000; now he was getting twice that plus £8,000 relocation expenses. As far as he was concerned, the contractual negotiations could be limited to a bit of small-talk and a smile.

He only had one good goalkeeper, Wilson explained, and even that one sometimes nearly gave him a heart attack, so uncertain was he when it came to dealing with crosses. Lars would be in competition with David Watson, the current number one. He was glad to hear it, said Lars. He was, after all, number two to Dirk Heinen at Leverkusen – whatever he did he was never going to get past him.

'Let's make it a three-year contract,' suggested chairman Dennis.

'Two years would be better,' said Lars, though he would curse himself for that two years later. At the time he was thinking that he didn't want to tie himself down for too long. First he wanted to see whether he and his family could settle down properly.

'So this contract is valid both for the First Division and the Premier League?' Lars continued. He was remembering how he had sat there trembling a year ago when it looked as though Leverkusen might be relegated.

Whatever division in the world Barnsley played in, said Dennis, the contract was still valid.

Barely half an hour after their arrival at Oakwell, Lars and Tony Woodcock were on their way back to Manchester.

An everyday football transfer had been drawn up; a player had just committed himself to two years without knowing whether his new club would be playing in the Premier League or the First Division, without knowing the town he would be moving to. All Lars knew for certain was that from 1 July 1997 Barnsley would be paying him good money and giving him his big chance to play professional football. The club had just invested a quarter of a million pounds in a player none of them had ever seen in a match. On top of that £250,000 transfer fee, Woodcock got a five-figure seem by way of commission for his efforts. Over three quarters of a million marks – no Bundesliga club had ever paid as much for a third-choice goalkeeper. But then, in Barnsley they thought he was a second-choice goalkeeper.

At Leverkusen, most of Lars' colleagues greeted the news of his move with amazement. In 1997 there was a lot of talk about player transfers between the big leagues in Germany, Italy, England and Spain; it was round about then that football clubs started operating internationally in the grand style. But more than half of it was empty talk. Only one German was playing in England in the spring of 1997 – the former GDR international Uwe Rösler with First Division Manchester City – so it was strange that a goal-keeper who wasn't in a Bundesliga line-up, and strictly speaking didn't even have a place on the subs' bench, was to be the second. 'Who did they get you mixed up with?' Leverkusen striker Eric Meijer asked his friend.

The Bayer Leverkusen players were in a good mood as the season came to an end. The year before they had finished two points ahead of relegated Kaiserslautern in the Bundesliga, and now they were two points behind the cham-pions, Bayern Munich. Rarely has a failure to win the cham-pionship been celebrated in the way that second place was fêted in Leverkusen. The whole team had to go out on to the balcony of the town hall and wave at the thousands of fans down below in the square. Lars squashed himself in behind his team-mates in the back row. It was a fantastic party, but it was embarrassing to allow himself to be applauded for something to which he had contributed nothing apart from an easy-going temperament during training. In 1997/98 he wanted to achieve more. His heart was set on playing at least one game as a professional.

In mid-May, he called Barnsley to find out whether he was going to be moving to the Premier League or the First Division. Woodcock had told him, 'That'll be decided by today's game. If they win against Bradford, they'll go up.' When Lars dialled the number, he discovered that the telephone in Barnsley's office was permanently engaged. Either someone had taken the phone off the hook because they hadn't made it, or people were constantly ringing up to congratulate them on their promotion. After half an hour, Lars finally got through. He didn't have to ask; the noise level at the other end told him all he needed to know. It sounded as though thousands of people were chanting at one another, 'We are Premier League, say we are Premier League!' Then there was a strange crash in the background, as though thousands of people were clinking and dropping beer-bottles. In fact, that was exactly what was happening in Barnsley that night. The bin-men would pick up 14 tons of broken glass the following morning.

5

THE GERMAN GIANT

THE NEWS OF Barnsley's promotion spread like wildfire. There were no season tickets left for 1997/98; there were only 37 season tickets left; there were 1,000 season tickets left; the club was going to build a new stand to make room for everyone. Michael Spinks, the club secretary, was fighting a lonely losing battle against such rumours. 'Advance sales haven't even started,' he protested.

Talk about painting a town red; pregnant women went shopping in their red nylon Barnsley shirts; schoolchildren wore their red woollen Barnsley scarves around their necks when it was 75 degrees outside; homeless people begged in the pedestrian precinct with red Barnsley baseball caps on. Barnsley had been playing football for 110 years, but from 9 August 1997 they were playing in the Premier League for the first time. The city was caught up in a frenzy of anticipation. 'The summer of 1997 was the summer of gold,' said Ian McMillan, the local poet. Just as towns employ town clerks, Barnsley had employed McMillan, after their promotion, as 'the world's first professional football poet', asking him to record their first Premier League season in a volume of poems. 'It was a time of great optimism,' McMillan remembered. 'Barnsley rose to the Premier League, Tony Blair and the Labour Party won the elections. And a third thing happened – but I can't remember what it was.'

The last time the rest of Great Britain had paid any attention to Barnsley was in 1984, when the coal-mining unions, led by the radical trade unionist Arthur Scargill, rose up in bitter protest at the policies of Margaret Thatcher. The miners' strike didn't save the coal-mines; on the contrary, in the end it only hastened their closure. Some 30,000 workers lost their jobs. A whole region lost its livelihood.

It was clear that the two events – the end of coal-mining and promotion to the Premier League – would be brought together in the media. Putting sport in a social context was a big journalistic fashion of the nineties. After all the years of bitterness, a smile was finally returning to the face of that poor, dirty, working-class town – that was the main thrust of articles, from the tabloids to the broadsheets, describing the miraculous rise of Barnsley's footballers.

Twelve years after the Iron Lady had left Barnsley shattered, the six per cent unemployment rate was still considerably higher than the national average of 3.6 per cent. According to a study by the European Union, South Yorkshire was one of the poorest regions in western Europe, on a par with Sicily and Estremadura in Spain. But by the summer of 1997, despite all its problems, Barnsley had been heading towards recovery for some time. Most of the 200,000 inhabitants had started new lives, like Andrew Mills, Lars' neighbour on Winter Avenue, who had once earned his living as a mining engineer; he now worked in Barnsley General Hospital as a nurse in the intensive ward. New opportunities were opening up, and the run-down, sooty town that still existed in the minds of most English people was in fact by now a clean market town in a beautiful hilly landscape. What Barnsley actually was, and will always remain, is provincial. Before 1992, if you lived there, television was as close as you got to the excitement of the world. But all of a sudden Barnsley itself was exciting. People went around shouting about it. It only took one person with a few pints under his belt to start up the chant in the market square and there would be dozens joining in all the way down Wellington Street, all through those long summer nights: 'We are Premier League, say we are Premier League!'

The Premiership itself was enjoying its great boom, and most stadiums were packed to the rafters every Saturday. Apart from speed and passion, the traditional ingredients of the English game, the matches were increasingly demonstrating high levels of technical skill, and pin-ups such as David Beckham and Michael Owen were fascinating to all social classes all around the world. In Australia and Norway, people would soon be switching on their televisions and watching Barnsley. In those circumstances, there can't have been many people in Barnsley who wouldn't want to say in years to come, 'I was there in the Premier League year 1997/98.'

Ian McMillan got up at twenty past five. He'd be at Oakwell by about six o'clock – that was sure to be early enough, three and a half hours before the cash-desks opened on that late May morning for the season-ticket sale. It was three and a half miles from his house to the stadium. McMillan walked it. He wanted to enjoy the quiet morning as well as its festive atmosphere – the feeling that great times were about to begin. McMillan was a long way from the prevailing image of the poet at the end of the twentieth century – someone living withdrawn from the world in an ivory tower, immersed in his art. McMillan was a story-teller in the medieval sense, solidly rooted in the life of his home town. He wrote poems about Barnsley, and on Friday evenings he went to the pubs, among the people, to deliver his poetry in his rich, deep voice. In a town in which only a minority would list reading as one of their hobbies, the people knew and loved him. He had grown up with them, he'd been going to the stadium with them for decades. He was one of them, even if he did wear garish Hawaiian shirts most people in Barnsley wouldn't even have put on a scarecrow, and said things they would never have dreamed of: 'When I see *Hamlet* in the theatre, I really enjoy it, but I know what happens in the end. With football you have no idea, that's the great thing about it.'

At ten to six, McMillan got his first view of Oakwell. When he reached the car park, he stopped. He had to: the car park in front of him was already packed with 3,000 people. He'll never forget the sight – a car park at six o'clock in the morning full of patient, good-humoured people. 'That was it: Barnsley in the Premier League. A town queuing up for the good times.'

Lars Leese couldn't really have found a better, more appropriate place than Barnsley, a club and a town heading feverishly towards their first appearances in the great world of football just as cluelessly, just as innocently, as he was. Except, of course, Barnsley hadn't brought him there because he was just as inexperienced and excited as everyone else in the club. Lars Leese was 'the German giant', as the *Barnsley Chronicle* announced at the beginning of June, one of those stars who would walk out of the television set and satisfy a provincial town's longing for flesh-and-blood idols. His arrival was the signal that they belonged among the greats. The leading English clubs had been employing foreign stars for two or three years: Chelsea had the Italians Gianluca Vialli and Gianfranco Zola, Arsenal had the Dutchmen Dennis Bergkamp and Marc Overmars, Manchester United had the Dane Peter Schmeichel. Barnsley needed some too. All teams in the Premier League had their international stars. Now they had their own; a giant goalkeeper from the country of the European champions.

'Barnsley was always a monocultural town. There are no blacks, and the only Asians are a few doctors and people with corner shops,' said McMillan. 'And all of a sudden these players from around the world were coming to Barnsley. It was exotic, it was exciting – Barnsley as an international hub. I, for example, had this daft idea of a map of the world in my head, and all the arrows pointed to Barnsley.'

In addition to Lars, Danny Wilson bought the Slovenian Ales Krizan, the Macedonian Georgi Hristov and the South African Eric Tinkler, and later in the season the Swede Peter Markstedt and the Norwegian Jan Aage Fjörtoft. Wilson justified himself by saying that the prices of English footballers had been going through the ceiling; abroad, he paid only half the equivalent transfer fee for players of the same quality. But that explanation couldn't get rid of the impression that Wilson was, like a child in a toyshop, enjoying the fact that he was finally employing foreign stars – or rather players who were foreign and were therefore seen as stars in Barnsley. Of all the imports, only Tinkler, who had played a minor role with Cagliari in Italy's Serie A, was known outside his country's borders. And even then, hardly anyone had heard of him. But that was the great thing about it, said McMillan. 'You'd have seen a British player at one time or another, you'd know something about him. We knew nothing at all about those foreign players. They could be anything. We could dream that they were going to be absolutely fantastic.'

The first bit of Lars Leese Barnsley saw was his legs. Then they looked up, higher and higher – did this guy reach the sky? Some 10,000 fans had turned up for the traditional open day about five weeks before the start of the season, their first opportunity to see the new players. When Lars walked along in front of the stadium stands, signing one autograph after another, a murmur followed him. Three centimetres short of two metres, he was. *Fuckin' hell! Six feet five!* For the time being, that was all they needed to know; he was going to be a giant goalkeeper. The photographer from the *Barnsley Chronicle* took the smallest child in the vicinity and put him next to the German to make it clear to every single reader what kind of sportsman Barnsley were dealing with here. When Ian McMillan saw the picture in the paper at the barber's, he went home and started his job as the world's first football poet:

> Lars Leese, tall as trees
> that grow in Wombwell Wood.
> Lars Leese, listen please:
> We think you're very good.

A few months later, McMillan fell silent for a moment when I pointed out to him that in German 'Leese' doesn't rhyme with 'trees', but he soon bounced back. For simplicity's sake, that was exactly how Lars pronounced his surname when he was in England.

The unconditional adulation Lars received immediately after his arrival in Barnsley was everything he had ever dreamed of. But it was frightening at the same time. The expectations that came with adoration kept him going even when he was asleep. The night before the first day of training, Lars and Daniela were in the Ardsley House Hotel because their house in Winter Avenue wasn't ready. Some time after midnight, Daniela woke up. Lying beside her, her husband stretched his arms up, then moved them to the right, dropped them, threw his head and body to the left, and pulled his arms back up again. He was catching balls in his sleep.

But he needn't have worried, at least so far as his first day of training was concerned: he never caught sight of a ball. Danny Wilson just made them run around the pitch. In the dressing-room the manager had introduced all the new players, but there were no long speeches; they'd all waited long enough for the season, it was time for things to get going. As they'd filed out, Malcolm Shotton, the reserve-team coach, had asked Lars whether he had any problems with running. For a goalkeeper he'd actually always been quite good at it, Lars replied. Just as well.

A hill led down from the training ground to the adjoining green meadows and hills, then down to a little pond at the bottom. A pithead could be seen in the distance, a left-over from the abandoned Barnsley II coal-mine, and then the hill led up to the stadium. When they'd run a few circuits, Lars joked with his new team-mates that Germans trained much harder. He knew the clichés the English liked hearing about Germans.

After an hour he'd stopped joking. They were still running. And after that, more running: this time speed-work, down to the pond and back in groups of four, about ten minutes a circuit, then a minute's break before moving off again. Under Christoph Daum all Lars had done on his first day's training was stimulate his muscles with light weights in the gym and get his body slowly accustomed to the strains it would shortly be subjected to. Elsewhere in the Premier League fitness coaches were moving in to lick the professionals into shape with scientifically worked-out programmes involving running and weights. At Barnsley, Danny Wilson followed the good old principle that a lot helps a lot. 'Run your bollocks off!'

Lars soon felt his strength giving out. He was actually running uphill, but he couldn't have been slower if he'd been walking. Every now and again the cry 'Rory, Rory!' rang out – a player who still had a bit of puff encouraging Rory Prendergast, a 19-year-old new recruit who couldn't play football terribly well but who ran like Speedy Gonzales. Prendergast overtook everyone else one after the other, running like a lunatic. 'At Leverkusen the senior pros would have yanked that guy back by his collar,' Lars thought to himself, hopelessly wishing that someone would wade in and stop this madness. After two hours – or was it three? He had lost all sense of time – they were finally allowed to sit down. And do 200 sit-ups. 'Ninety per cent of headers are won with the stomach muscles,' explained Malcolm Shotton, and no one had the courage, let alone the strength, to contradict him.

Ashen-faced, Lars drove back to the hotel. He went to bed convinced he would never be able to move again.

The next day they trained exactly the same way all over again.

Apart from an ache in muscles he didn't know he had, during those first training days Lars sensed that not everyone at Barnsley was enthusiastic about the arrival of these supposed international stars. The English players weren't exactly falling over themselves to welcome them into the team. Before their first day's training the new foreign players, even though they didn't know one another, had sat down one after the other on the short bench nearest the door of the dressing-room; the established local players sat on the long bench opposite. It was the classic seating arrangement of a modern football team. In top teams like Leverkusen, where the local players had got used to the presence of foreigners over the years and most of the overseas stars had played in several countries, the professionals know how to get along with one another; at Barnsley, on the other hand, foreigners who had never played abroad before (apart from Eric Tinkler) were being thrown into a team that had until then been almost exclusively British. The invisible dividing line that passed through the room between the two sets of players would never really be crossed during the next two years.

The envy of the English players caught me unawares. I had planned to conform, to fit in, apart from anything else because I've always liked the feeling of belonging that you get in football. But I was irritated at feeling rejected like that. Today, I wonder: 'Should we foreigners have been more stubborn about trying to make contact with the others?' Perhaps we were too aloof. Every time the English laughed and we didn't know what was going on – and at first, with their strong accents, we hardly understood a thing – we thought they were laughing at us. Automatically, as though it was inevitable, the team split into two groups: on the bus the foreigners sat at the front, the English at the back. David Watson and I were the exceptions. Goalkeepers have a natural bond with one another. David and I respected each other as goalkeepers, so we stuck together. I can even understand the envy of the Englishmen: the

promotion was their doing, and all of a sudden you had all these guys coming from all over the place – Slovenia, Slovakia or whatever it was called – and fighting them for places in the line-up. And then you had the fact that we foreigners were much better paid. There were players on the team, regular players from the promotion squad like Adrian Moses or Martin Bullock, who maybe got just £2,000 a month. I was on £2,000 a *week*, and of the four foreigners who arrived at the start of the season I was still the one on the lowest wages. But isn't everyone responsible for his own contract? Why didn't they go straight to the chairman and say, 'Fuckin' hell, why are the fuckin' foreigners earning so much more?' Instead they just went to the toilet and complained about us. Once, Darren Barnard and Adie Moses were standing in the urinal laughing, and when I came in they immediately fell silent.

Manager Danny Wilson told the *Barnsley Chronicle* about the difficulties involved in integrating a large group of foreign players. 'Some foreigners came to England with the wrong attitude,' he said, talking about the Premier League in general. At Barnsley, on the other hand, everything was fine. 'Here, it's one for all and all for one,' the manager said, and very few fans and readers doubted Wilson. He still had such an innocent smile on his boyish face.

In the pre-season training camp in Exeter, Wilson introduced a novel exercise to boost team spirit: he let the team spend an evening in the beer garden. The foreigners sat at one end of the table, the Englishmen at the other. Even so, said goalkeeper David Watson, that evening they learned a bit more about one another. 'Presumably the foreigners were surprised at the amount we drank,' he said. Not really: on the continent it was well known that many English professionals thought it was all part of a good night out to down nine or ten pints of beer. What amazed Lars was that they never had to go to the toilet. He had drunk four beers and been to the gents several times. 'How do they do that?' he wondered. He worked it out when he heard a splashing noise under the table; midfielder Darren Sheridan had rolled up one leg of his shorts and was watering the grass under the table. Above the table he went on talking as though nothing was happening.

Wilson had chosen Exeter because the place brought them luck. It was there that Barnsley had prepared themselves the previous summer for the season that led to their promotion. Lars, of course, fully understood all kinds of superstition, but even he wondered whether this was how things should be. Here was Barnsley Football Club, promoted to the richest league in the world, making its players, who earned up to £4,000 a week, stay in a students' residence. They had their meals in the student canteen, their only company a few students who had stayed on despite the holidays and some tourists who rented the bare single rooms – bed, table, washbasin, cupboard, no television; a shower and a toilet were on the landing – for a tenner a night.

In terms of quality, the pitch was much like the accommodation, but at least the training filled Lars with confidence this time. Wilson demonstrated a good eye for tactical details and tried out various different formations. The season had finally got under way.

It was a time of great innocence. A few months later some people in Barnsley would start quietly wondering whether naivety might not have been a more accurate word. But in the golden summer of 1997, Barnsley, both club and town, was a bastion of loveable romanticism. Danny Wilson said there was no point just talking about staying in the league; he couldn't rule out a place among the top six. 'People might laugh, but why shouldn't we reach for the stars?' he said. Keith Lodge, who had been writing about the club for decades with cool, dignified irony in the *Barnsley Chronicle*, captured the sense of expectation: 'With Moses standing proudly in the middle of a heaving red sea of expectant humanity, Oakwell was the perfect setting for another miracle,' he wrote. He was referring to Adrian Moses, not the Old Testament prophet.

The club sold 16,000 season tickets and had to send several thousand fans away empty-handed; the remaining 2,800 places in the stadium were reserved for the supporters of the opposing team. But on 10 July Barnsley folk were queuing again in the middle of the night; the next morning would see Premier League replica shirts go on sale for the first time. The club shop printed a batch of T-shirts with the legend I QUEUED FOR BARNSLEY to celebrate. In the end, so many fans turned up that merchandising manager Clive Wood joked that they should have done another batch reading I QUEUED FOR AN 'I QUEUED FOR BARNSLEY' T-SHIRT.

Ian McMillan went with his daughter to a pre-season friendly in nearby Doncaster. His daughter was wearing the red shirt, number 21, TINKLER over her shoulders. They watched Georgi Hristov, Barnsley's £1.5 million Macedonian, trying to wangle himself a penalty by taking a theatrical dive. 'Fuckin' hell, what's that?' Barnsley's English subs wondered on the bench, but the poet thought to himself, 'What a fantastic dive! That's new, that's good, we're Premier League.'

Lars received an invitation from the travel agency Going Places. He was to open a new branch in the pedestrian precinct. When he walked through the town centre with Daniela a few days before the opening was due to take place and saw a series of neon-yellow posters advertising the event, he felt quite strange. COMING SOON − RE-OPENING WITH STAR GUEST LARS LEESE they said. Lars thought to himself, 'No one's going to go to that.' He persuaded the Slovenian defender Ales Krizan to come along so that he wouldn't end up sitting on his own in the empty shop.

If the substitute goalkeeper of a Bundesliga club opened a shop, people would look at the poster and think, 'They've got the cheapest celebrity they could find.' And then they would walk past. When I turned up with Ales at Going Places ten minutes before the agreed time, there was already a queue of up to a hundred people stretching into the street. They'd come just to see me cut through a stupid blue ribbon. When I got out of the shop with Ales a couple of hours and a hundred autographs later, we were both overwhelmed. What on earth was going to happen, we wondered, on the first day of the season?

A hundred red and white balloons rose from the pitch, and Chumbawamba roared out of the Oakwell speakers: 'Oh Danny Boy, Danny Boy − I get knocked down, but I get up again . . .' Just half an hour to go until Barnsley's first Premier League kick-off.

In the dressing-room, striker Paul Wilkinson was in the bathtub.

'What are you doing?' asked Lars, dumbfounded.

'Warming up,' said Wilkinson.

'In the tub?'

'It's hot water.'

Lars looked at him. Wilkinson was quite serious. He was lying in hot water to warm up. And no one seemed to see anything extraordinary in that.

The sun was shining when the Barnsley and West Ham players stepped out of the dark tunnel below the grandstand. Most of the Barnsley players stared at the ground, as though they were afraid of being blown away if they looked up at the packed terraces, into the eye of that noisy, cheering hurricane.

Lars took his seat on the subs' bench. For the moment he was happy to let Watson have the position between the posts without a struggle. Because his transfer hadn't been dealt with quickly enough by the German Football Association during the summer holidays, he hadn't been able to play any kind of a warm-up match until just a few days earlier. And the experience of playing in that reserve-team friendly had taught him humility. As soon as he caught the ball for the first time he went to roll it out to the nearest of his team-mates, as goalkeepers do in Germany, but the ball went straight into touch. The team-mate Lars was trying to play to had been running forward at the time without so much as a glance at the goalkeeper. On other occasions Lars' defenders lost control of the ball as soon as Lars passed it to them; several opposition players would hurl themselves at the defender all at the same time. 'Kick the fuckin' ball into the fuckin' channel!' Malcolm Shotton shouted to Lars. When one of his defenders once again lost a ball that had been rolled to him, and Shotton looked as though he was about to explode on the sidelines, it occurred to Lars that English and German footballers played very differently. Here, they didn't give the opposing team any time to build a game slowly from inside their own half. The opponents applied such pressure that neither team could catch its breath until it managed to work the ball at least into midfield. This fast and impetuous style of play wasn't entirely to Lars' liking. So he was happy for David Watson to have first go for the time being. Lars would watch the whole thing and enjoy the atmosphere. He'd get his chance sooner or later.

Only one of the much-awaited foreigners, the South African Tinkler, was in the side to play West Ham. To Danny Wilson, loyalty was one of the most important virtues in football; the heroes of Barnsley's promotion at least deserved the chance to prove themselves in the top league. West Ham, who had for years epitomised mediocrity within the Premier League, seemed like an ideal first opponent.

After just nine minutes of Premier League football in Barnsley, defender Nicky Eaden sent a high cross deep into West Ham's penalty area. Attacker Paul Wilkinson – the one in the bath – was level with the far post and headed the ball not at the goal but diagonally, back towards Eaden. It's the simplest trick in the world, but every weekend it works in some football stadium somewhere: Wilkinson pulled the defender back with him, creating space at the near post, and Barnsley's captain Neil Redfearn steamed into the gap to head Wilkinson's lay-off powerfully into the goal.

People who have played hundreds of football matches may not remember all that many results, but they will have a memory of certain moments, snapshots that remain frozen for ever in their mind's eye. Neil Redfearn darting away from the goal, his right arm, the one with the captain's armband, stretched crookedly into the sky, index finger first, and behind him on the steeply raked stands 4,000 red shirts leaping into the air, a red wall, open-mouthed – it's an image that no one lucky enough to be at Oakwell that day will ever forget. Even ten years later the mere memory of it will bring back the same goosepimples, the same lump in the throat as it did then. The moment when Oakwell believed in the existence of paradise.

Of course, it wasn't to be. By 4.45 Barnsley had lost their Premier League première 2–1. Not much had been missing, just the crucial ingredient: hard-headedness. It was the beginning of August, almost 80 degrees, and the *Sunday Telegraph* prophesied: 'Barnsley face a long, hard winter.'

David Watson, who hadn't been able to conceal his nerves all afternoon, had West Ham's equalising goal on his conscience, having run out to take a cross he was never going to reach. On the subs' bench disappointment mingled with the merest hint of personal satisfaction. 'Another two or three mistakes like that and it'll be my turn,' Lars thought to himself.

'No one's going to go to Barnsley and have an easy game,' West Ham's manager Harry Redknapp generously said at the press conference after his team's victory. A fortnight later Chelsea came to Barnsley and won 6–0. The fans let the players hear what they thought of it. They sang 'Always Look on the Bright Side of Life'. And, two minutes before the final whistle, they chanted 'We're going to win 7–6.' Sky Television broadcast the match live, and Barnsley got its chance to speak to the nation: This season is our party; we're to enjoy it, whatever happens to us. From what they'd seen that afternoon, the whatever was likely to be bad.

Lars, who had been watching the supporters more closely than the match from his position on the subs' bench, could hardly believe his eyes. He was so impressed by the spectators' demonstration of good humour that he broke a taboo: he made contact with the fans on his own initiative. Professionals never do anything like that; they politely fulfil demands for autographs, switch on their smiles for a photograph after the match, and that's it. But Lars logged on to the unofficial Barnsley website, www.redders.co.uk, and wrote to tell the fans that he'd never seen anything like it. 'In Germany,' he wrote, 'you'd lock yourself in your house after a 6–0 defeat for fear of riots. In Barnsley, you can go out and be drunk in an hour because everyone wants to buy you a beer in consolation.'

Generally, though, Lars didn't need to seek contact with the fans. They came to his house. The news that a star was living in Winter Avenue in Royston quickly did the rounds. Children hung around outside his house just to be near him, and every half an hour one of them plucked up the courage to ring the doorbell and ask for an autograph. On 18 August, Lars ate his dinner in shifts. In between, he kept going to the door to sign autographs and make small-talk. It was his 28th birthday.

That was one evening when I thought, 'Can't they leave me in peace?' But then I said to myself, 'What can visitor number 101 do about the fact that a hundred others have rung the bell before he did?' I've never forgotten chasing after the stars as a child. On Saturdays I was often a ball-boy at FC Cologne. After every game I asked the goalkeepers if I could have their gloves – I never got them. I wanted to do it better than the other goalkeepers had. I made a resolution: never be unfriendly to the fans.

Daniela thought this was fine, as resolutions went. But did he really have to talk to everybody, run to the door at the slightest sound? 'You've got to draw a line somewhere,' she thought. Once they went dancing in the Barnsley nightclub Hedonism. It was the last time, Daniela promised herself.

She stood forlornly in the wings all evening while fans dashed up to her husband to talk about Barnsley's chances of staying in the Premier League. Finally, Lars fled with her on to the dance floor. Everyone else immediately stopped dancing. They stood around the couple in a circle 'and stared at us as though Frank Sinatra had shown up in the club', Daniela recalled.

She crept around in her house. The world outside seemed hostile and inaccessible to her. 'You've just got to get out there and stand up for yourself,' said Lars, very much in the style of a football coach. But he understood that it must be hard for his wife. He was kept busy through football and he made acquaintances through his job, but Daniela had ended up all alone in an introverted provincial town in a foreign country. She barely understood the language in any case, but Barnsley accents were completely beyond her.

Unhappy wives are just as much a part of modern football as fat wage packets and refined marking techniques, yet a professional can expect nothing but hysterical laughter from the fans and mocking headlines in the papers if he explains that he's transferred from one club to another because his wife is miserable in a little town in Germany or some rain-drenched Scottish backwater. Anyone would understand an argument like that if it came from, say, an architect explaining why he had moved from Wolfsburg or Kilmarnock. But in professional football this kind of explanation has too often been abused. When players say, 'My wife isn't happy here,' they often mean, 'I can earn more money elsewhere.' Modern football has produced several such phrases with hidden meanings. 'I just need a new challenge,' players say when they are switching from a top club to a mediocre team; what they mean is: 'At the top club I wouldn't have been a regular fixture in the side next season.' 'I've always wanted to go abroad' means 'I'm 33 and I'd never get a three-year contract here because everyone knows my knees are knackered.' 'In football the manager is always right' means 'When in God's name are they going to get around to firing this bloke?'

Ian McMillan's daughter asked him cautiously about the 6–0 Chelsea defeat. 'Wouldn't it be better to be back playing in the First Division, and win every now and again?' she said. But there was no time to be gloomy. Three days later they were due to play their next game, against Bolton Wanderers. This was the match in which goalkeeper Watson was so badly injured that Lars was forced into an eagerly awaited debut – once he'd managed to tie his laces. Two of the new boys, Eric Tinkler and Georgi Hristov, scored the goals that brought them a 2–1 victory, and 'everything was rosy again', said McMillan. Four games in, Barnsley was tenth among the 20 teams in the Premiership.

David Watson was out of the game for three weeks after the Bolton game, 'but the feeling, the innocent feeling was: Lars'll sort things out,' McMillan recalled. 'After all, he's from the German league.' And after his performance in that match, even Lars could get some sleep the night before the following match in Derby. He now knew he was capable of playing at that level. For safety's sake, though, he said it to himself a few times out loud before he made his first start in a professional game at Pride Park in front of 27,200 spectators: 'You can do it. You can do it.'

Barnsley lost the game 1–0, the result of a penalty given against Lars for a late tackle on Derby County's striker Francesco Baiano. That's what they'll put in the record books, but as far as Lars was concerned, it was perhaps the best game he had played in the whole of his career.

The match itself was too unspectacular, the result too frustrating, for anyone to remember Lars' performance as being particularly noteworthy, but if he focused on his own actions and blanked out everything else, Lars knew he'd had a fantastic game. He stopped one lone attack by Baiano with such an amazing reflex save that the Italian automatically held out his hand in congratulation. He caught crosses so easily in mid-air that team captain Redfearn asked him the next morning, 'Did you spend the night in the greenhouse?' And he wasn't entirely to blame for the penalty that had, strictly speaking, been his fault: Baiano had already dribbled his way through Barnsley's defence and no goalkeeper could have reached the ball at his feet; tripping up the Italian was the only thing Lars could do to stop him scoring. Back home in Cologne, *Bild* ran a story on Lars under the headline FOOT-BALLING FAIRY-TALE IN ENGLAND. Danny Wilson told Lars, 'Go on like that, and you'll stay number one.'

6

THE GOALKEEPER

On his back he wears number one. The first to get paid?
The first to pay! The goalkeeper's always to blame.
    — from 'The Goalkeeper' by Eduardo Galeano

THERE ARE GOOD reasons for becoming a goalkeeper:
you're not good enough to play in the outfield. You're
too easy-going to say no when everyone else refuses.

Lars Leese was too tall as a child.

The tallest one always had to go in goal.

Later, when they've spent a few years between the posts and
may even be making a bravura performance of it, some goalkeepers maintain that they love the position. They're pretending. The next time they let in a goal, they know that themselves.

From that point on they're on their own.

Few people are as lonely as the goalkeeper in a stadium
filled with thousands of spectators when the other side has
scored. If a striker bungles his third chance, his team-mates
slap him on the bum and say, 'Come on, the fourth one'll
go in.' When the goalkeeper makes three fantastic saves and

lets in the fourth, a barely saveable shot, the midfield player says to the striker, 'How are we going to win if that guy at the back keeps lobbing balls into the net all by himself?'

Lars Leese lay on the ground during his third professional game for Barnsley, against Aston Villa, and when he lifted his head all he could see was his team-mates turning away from him. Mark Draper, Villa's peroxided midfielder, had charged alone towards Lars; there'd been no sign of Barnsley's defence. Draper slatted the ball straight between Lars' legs into the net. The final score was 3–0 to Villa, and the German football magazine *kicker* reported: 'Leese allowed a shot from Draper to trickle in between his legs.'

In fact, Lars had done everything he possibly could. If the attacker is standing alone in front of him, the goalkeeper must be ready to jump to either side, so he stands there legs akimbo; the percentage shot for the attacker in such a situation is to aim between the goalkeeper's legs because he can rarely get his feet together quickly enough. But most spectators just see the goalkeeper looking awkward, not to say clumsy, pulling his legs together in a panic, possibly losing his balance and landing on his bottom. In their heads, the majority of the spectators are defenders, midfielders or strikers.

When the keeper gets his fingertips to a ball heading for the top corner of the net with an enormous leap, the spectators are amazed – that's a great keeper. On the other hand, if a keeper throws himself on a perfectly normal shot that's bounced up six feet in front of him on a wet pitch, no one applauds. And yet that's the one that's much harder to save. The goalkeeper has only a fraction of a second to gauge whether the ball's bouncing in the wrong direction off the damp grass, and he doesn't know whether or

**not it will be too slippery to catch. The spectators
hiss when a goalkeeper wallops a back-pass way into
touch and the television commentators moan, 'He's
not much of a ball-player, is he?' What I maintain is
that that's exactly what makes a good goalkeeper.
Every now and again he must hoof the ball into the
stand; he doesn't try to please the public, he just tries
to find the safest option. Anyone can dive across goal
and turn a ball round the post with their fingertips.**

Some goalkeepers, thirsty for recognition, have tried to win
the public over with breathtaking stunts. Bundesliga goalkeepers like Andreas Köpke of FC Nuremberg, a European
Championship winner with Germany in 1996, Uwe Kamps
of Borussia Mönchengladbach and Raimond Aumann of
Bayern Munich would swing from the cross-bar after a save,
like Tarzan on a vine. They dramatically punched away shots
they should have been able to catch, and before diving to
their right they first took a step to the left to make the leap
look even more spectacular. In order to win the admiration
of the public they ran the risk of being despised by their own
profession. They have sold out, grumble their peers.
Goalkeepers' heroes are men like Stefan Klos of Glasgow
Rangers or Frank Rost of Werder Bremen, matter-of-fact
craftsmen who strive for perfect positional play rather than
dazzling saves.

Rarely does a goalkeeper impress everyone, his colleagues
as well as the public, but Oliver Kahn managed it in 2001.
Bild called him the 'titanic keeper' after he helped Bayern
Munich win the German championship and the Champions
League, and he was crowned Footballer of the Year by a
massive margin – around 80 per cent of German sports journalists voted for him. The goalkeeping fraternity felt it was

a victory for all of them. Kahn may have been the best, but at the same time he was only one of them; at last they'd got the recognition they deserved. A striker like Oliver Bierhoff needed only two goals in the 1996 European Championship final, one of them a lucky shot, to win mass adoration and advertising contracts; a goalkeeper like Oliver Kahn had to go on making world-class saves for five years before he achieved a similar status. And for the first four years his obsessive facial expressions and muscular physique meant he was known only as a crazed gorilla. In the great flood of interviews Kahn gave after he won his unexpected fame, he revealed that even the most confident goalkeeper in the world rarely enjoys a football match. 'If anyone knows fear, then I do,' Kahn told the Berlin *Tagesspiegel*. 'Fear of failure, fear of defeat. You can't think clearly. It completely tenses you up.'

Great writers like Albert Camus and Vladimir Nabokov have been goalkeepers. That feeds the myth that goalkeepers have the position of the calm, intelligent, chosen one. (The truth is, I'm afraid, that Camus and Nabokov just couldn't hack it on the field.) But it is clear that the goalkeeper is something special in a football team: he's the only one who's allowed to touch the ball with his hands for a start. So it's all the more surprising that the value of a good keeper has never really been acknowledged. Salaries decline from attack to midfield to defence, and the goalkeeper is left with only scraps. Of course, Oliver Kahn is one of the best-paid professionals at Bayern Munich, but that exception doesn't prove anything. Kahn, the best goalkeeper in the world, still doesn't earn half as much as Zinedine Zidane, Luis Figo, Alessandro del Piero or Ronaldo, some of the best-known attacking players in the world. It makes you wonder whether the people sitting in the boardrooms and offices of big clubs aren't just cool-headed directors but also childish fans who see the goal-chaser as

God and the goalkeeper as a mere necessity, tolerated at best.

All the goalkeeper can do is go on waiting in his penalty area, alone in his brightly coloured shirt – 'whose exuberant colours are supposed to console him for his loneliness', as the South American author Eduardo Galeano put it. In truth, it's not the shirt but the enormous gloves that are his best friend, his succour. Very few working people have such a profound relationship with the tools of their trade. It's impossible, for instance, to imagine a surgeon loving his scalpel the way a goalkeeper loves his gloves.

Pulling on his gloves is Lars Leese's favourite movement. Forcing his fingers through the tight elastic opening, then pulling the Velcro fastener shut – immediately he has the feeling of being strong and protected.

In summer, when it's dry, goalkeepers spit on their gloves to get a better grip on the ball. Toni Schumacher always chewed on a piece of chewing-gum because he thought the mixture of saliva and sugar had even better adhesive properties. Lars always kept a bottle of water behind the goal-line so that his mouth never dried up. But with or without chewing-gum, in the summer, when the ball and the grass are both dry, the ball slaps into a keeper's gloves and seems to want to stay there; it sticks to the soft foam rubber. It's only that sound of a dry ball slapping into spit-wetted gloves that makes the goalkeeper happy. That dull 'plop' gives him the sense that he's unbeatable, that he can catch any ball you can kick at him.

After training, Lars never went to the shower without his gloves. He painstakingly cleaned them by hand, with shampoo. The other goalkeepers at Barnsley, Watson and Anthony Bullock, the club's number three, looked at him with envy. Lars had gloves with his name on the Velcro. In Germany it was customary to provide that bit of extra service for professional goalkeepers. It wasn't the case in England. Lars could understand Watson's envy. The first time he got gloves with his name on in Leverkusen, he wore them all the way home.

I've been playing in goal for more than 20 years now. But do I like it? I don't know. Of course, as a goalkeeper you experience moments of total happiness – when you stop a shot that seemed unsaveable to the 18,000 spectators in the stadium. But if you bask in that feeling of happiness for more than a few seconds, you'll let a goal in, and no one will remember your save, just the mistake you made afterwards. They often say of strikers, 'You don't see him for 89 minutes, and then in the 90th he scores the winning goal.' And that's a compliment. But if you don't see a goalkeeper for 89 minutes, he'll have let in eight goals! If my fairy godmother were to come down now and say, 'Lars, I'm going to turn you into a world-class goalkeeper or a world-class striker – you can choose,' I'm not sure what I'd do. I've been a goalkeeper for so long that I identify with the position. But I still think I'd go for world-class striker.

Lars told himself that he didn't need to take the criticism in *kicker* seriously. He knew it wasn't true. Mark Draper's goal hadn't been his mistake, and the correspondent from the football magazine hadn't even seen the game. But then, no one in Germany had seen it; they'd only read about it in *kicker*. Werner Friese, his former goalkeeping coach at Leverkusen, phoned him. 'What kind of a soft goal did you let in, then?' he said. After the fourth phone call like that Lars found it hard to go on believing in his own blamelessness. Goalkeepers soon start to feel guilty. Their position encourages negative thinking. Nobody remembers a goalkeeper's saves; he's measured against his mistakes. 'The rest of the players can commit a terrible blunder here or there, but they erase it again with some spectacular dribbling or a masterful pass,' wrote Eduardo Galeano, 'but the goalkeeper can't do that. The crowd won't forgive the goalkeeper anything.'

Most goalkeepers try to protect themselves against the constant carping by being extremely self-critical. They are hard on themselves so that other people's criticism won't hurt as much. After every goal he conceded, Lars' first thought was always the same: you could have saved that one. Only after the game, when he was analysing those goals over and over again, would he sometimes admit: you couldn't have saved that shot with the best will in the world. But when people whose only knowledge of his 'error' came from reading *kicker* wanted to rub his nose in it, it was hard even for an optimist like Lars to maintain his own convictions.

If I'd had 200 Bundesliga matches behind me, I mightn't have cared so much about what was written about me. But I'd just played my third professional game. It was a completely new experience to have tens of thousands of people staring at my hands and journalists noting down every miskick. I knew I had to stop listening to what other people were saying, I had to blank it out and just get on with things. But things are never as simple as that. Oliver Kahn once said he liked having everyone against him, that it motivated him. I'm not like that. I need security. I have to know for myself: Lars, you're good. I have to be sure: Lars, your manager and your colleagues trust you. If he has that certainty, a goalkeeper can become a kind of avalanche; with every good game he keeps getting

bigger and bigger. At some point he's so huge that the strikers freeze in front of him. They wonder, 'How am I going to get the ball past him?' and shoot straight at him. That happened with Oliver Kahn. That's why it was interesting to read that even he was sometimes gripped with fear, suddenly, in the middle of a game. Fear comes completely unannounced and tries to strip you of all your self-confidence. Then you have to fight back. You just have to try like crazy.

Three days after the match against Aston Villa the opportunity came to fight back, to sweep away self-doubt. Barnsley were playing in the League Cup against Chesterfield. Twice the central defenders Peter Shirtliff and Adrian Moses shouted at Lars to come the fuck out of his area, but he stayed put. Barnsley won 2–1 against the Second Division club, and Lars was sure he'd made the right decision – not to dash 20 or 25 yards off his goal-line in an effort to clear through-balls as his defenders were telling him to do. Running too far out would just have been taking a stupid risk. Of course he would have looked fantastic if he'd actually got the ball in time and seen off the threat, but what would have happened if the attacker had got to the ball before he did? The danger of conceding a free-kick or, worse, missing the ball completely had been far too great. He wasn't a desperado. The other players didn't understand that good goalkeepers aren't impetuous.

After the match Lars sent an email to his father-in-law: 'So, at the weekend we're playing Everton. A huge game. If you could send me a shot of positive energy at three o'clock, I think that might help me a bit.'

That Sunday against Everton, David Watson was back in goal. Lars was flabbergasted. He didn't ask Danny Wilson the reason. It could only mean that the manager was unhappy with his game, but he couldn't afford to let that chip away at his frail self-confidence. So Lars looked for his own explanations. He pretended that things weren't as serious as all that. Perhaps Wilson had been irritated that he hadn't come off his line to clear those through-balls against Chesterfield. After all, the manager had never played in goal himself. At any rate, he hadn't done badly in his first four games, Lars thought, and against Derby he had even played very well. Now everyone could see whether David Watson could do any better.

Clearly, in the eyes of the manager he couldn't. A week later, a week that saw two games with eight goals conceded, Wilson put Lars back in goal. Then, two matches after that, it was Watson's turn again. 'I didn't get enough consistency from either of them,' Wilson explained. 'They were nervous during the matches, understandably enough, bearing in mind that they were both young goalkeepers, David in terms of his age, at 23, and Lars in terms of his professional experience. But we had no time to wait for them to find their feet. We were in the Premier League, and I needed a strong, confident goalkeeper – straight away.'

They were basically very different types of goalkeeper. Watson, only five feet ten inches tall, was quick on his feet. He usually took two or three little steps before launching himself at balls, and often he didn't dive at all, he just ran after the shots. Lars took huge leaps and stretched himself as much as he could, making use of that enormous span of his. Watson had incredible reflexes, Lars an extraordinary presence. It was time for them to show their strengths, Wilson thought. His idea was to force the goalkeepers into stiff competition with each other. By making first one play, then the other, he'd make them both hungry. As furious rivals, Watson and Lars would drive themselves on to higher and higher accomplishments.

In fact, the opposite happened. Wilson's policy of alternation had the effect of bringing the two goalkeepers closer together. Their initial respect for each other had first turned into real affection when Lars visited Watson in hospital the day after his accident during the Bolton match. He met Watson's mother in the waiting-room and said to her, 'Don't worry, your son's a better goalkeeper than I am.' 'Do you see?' asked Watson years later, visibly touched. 'The very fact that he came to the hospital! I'd been playing for eight years with some of my Barnsley colleagues, and Lars had only been there for two months, and he was the only one who visited me. And then he told my mother I was a better goalkeeper than he was! That tells you all you need to know about him. He's a sincere, honest guy.'

When the manager started to play them off against each other, they quickly agreed that things couldn't go on like that. Goalkeepers only get worse if the manager is forever switching them around. Wilson had to decide in favour of one or the other, even though Watson and Lars, quite naturally, had differing opinions on whom he should choose.

By switching us around all the time, the manager was giving the rest of the players an alibi: it made us goalkeepers responsible for any defeats. But by the time we lost 7–0 to Manchester United – and David couldn't have stopped a single one of those goals – it should have been clear to everyone that we goalkeepers weren't entirely to blame. Seven goals that no goalkeeper in the world would have had a hope of saving – what did that tell us about the defence? Certainly, neither David nor I had spectacular games during the first few weeks. Nonetheless, the manager should have chosen one or other of us

as his number one much earlier on. After six weeks of preparation, I should know, as a manager, which keeper I like better. It's strange that there are still managers who want to switch goalkeepers around the way you do with defenders. You should be able to see where that's headed: if there's no clear number one, after a few weeks both goalkeepers will be playing below standard. If you worry about getting chucked out of the team the next time you make a mistake, then you start making mistakes. Particularly as a goalkeeper, when you have so much time to think. It's as though you're in jail standing at the back there. You can't physically work off that tension. So many times I just wanted to run out of that penalty area and flatten somebody, take his feet out from under him. Maybe the ref will give you a yellow card, but you'll feel refreshed, released. The pressure's off. Outfield players are lucky to be able to do that.

Four years later, Danny Wilson smiled, good-humouredly, when I told him he'd achieved only one thing with his little scheme: he'd managed to unite the two goalkeepers against him. He had in fact noticed that himself. 'I wouldn't do it now,' he said, 'switching the goalkeepers around like that all the time. Goalkeepers are so alone – they need understanding, not harsh treatment. That's what I learned back then with Lars and David. I wanted to challenge their egoism, I wanted them to think, "The manager is giving me the chance to be number one, but I'm going to have to be ruthless to get there." But that wasn't the way they were thinking. David and Lars were two great guys, always prepared to listen, always willing to learn. I liked them. But as a football manager it's often easier if you have real bastards in the team.'

7

BARNSLEY BY NIGHT

IT WAS A cold, rainy Saturday night in Barnsley. Lars Leese and I stood out like sore thumbs. We were the only people wearing jackets or coats. Girls in sandals, no stockings or socks, with mini-skirts and midriff-revealing tops, both as tight as possible, were meeting boys in bright green or neon blue Yves Saint Laurent or Ralph Lauren shirts with razor-sharp creases which they wore outside their trousers, medium-sized gold rings in both ears and so much gel on their short hair that their scalps gleamed. This uniform was worn at weekends regardless of age or physique. The belly of a 50-year-old woman bulged between skirt and top. A girl of about 17 wore a mini-dress that hung limply from her body. Perhaps her breasts would grow into it in a couple of years. Many of the girls had their shoulders pulled forwards, their arms folded in front of their chests, in a bid to warm themselves up. 'Ooh, it's really cold,' they complained. They said it as though it was simply an unfortunate fact of life. Dressing warmly didn't seem to be an option. Later, a girl told me that she and her girlfriends always took flu tablets on Saturdays as a precaution before they went out.

As though in a wild procession, hundreds of them moved back and forth between the pubs and bars of the town centre in small, relaxed groups that were almost always exclusively female or exclusively male. Bars like Brownes had put speakers on their outside walls, and they bombarded the streets with relentless techno. Music from various establishments merged in the town centre into a confused, banging blanket of noise.

'One night in Bangkok makes a hard man tremble,' sang Murray Head in 1986. He'd had a big hit with it, but I was pretty sure he'd really had Barnsley in mind. At that time I didn't know that most towns in the north of England turned into party zones on weekend evenings, of the kind Germans only ever experience at carnival time – with the small difference that we go about the place in fancy dress at carnival, while northern girls seem to dress in as little as they possibly can.

Lars had promised to take me out one evening, 'because no one can believe what goes on here unless they've seen it with their own eyes'. I started to believe him long before we got to our actual destination, the Theatre nightclub on Wellington Street. By then we'd already been spontaneously asked as guests of honour to a wedding party in the Queen's Hotel, stopped to discuss Barnsley reserves' last few games with a couple of 16-year-old girls, and been invited by about 532 strangers to go for a beer. (We didn't accept all the invitations.)

The hospitality of the people of Barnsley to foreigners is warm enough already; if they know you've got a professional footballer standing beside you, it's overwhelming. True, enthusiasm for Barnsley FC had clear boundaries: it was limited to the town itself. Only 20 miles away, in Wakefield or Sheffield, hardly anyone would have turned to look at Lars. But in Barnsley, said manager Danny Wilson, 'the players lived in a goldfish bowl. They could hardly move, and their every move was the object of close attention.'

Not that some of the players minded too much. Clinton Marcelle, the little substitute striker from Trinidad, spent a few afternoons parked outside McDonald's on Market Hill in his open-top Mercedes SLK. Whenever he got bored, he would open and shut the roof over and over again. But mostly his car was surrounded by teenagers, and he was able to tell them how much his Mercedes had cost, that his suit was Versace, that he always flew first class to Trinidad so that he could stretch his legs. Given that he was only five foot six, that was a luxury even the kids may have found surprising.

With the exception of the Norwegian Jan Aage Fjörtoft, who moved to the club in January 1998, and, as a Norway regular, enjoyed great popularity at home, Barnsley's players were all journeyman professionals. Their only experience of mass adoration from the media was when they read reports about people like David Beckham and Ronaldo. Now they could be the David Beckham of Royston, the Ronaldo of Grimethorpe. Who could complain if they liked the attention?

But perhaps they didn't have to go looking for it quite as blatantly as Clinton Marcelle outside McDonald's.

Lars Leese always stood politely at the back of the queue outside a nightclub. It still struck him as peculiar to exploit the privileges of the small-town star, and simply to march past the waiting people into the club. Sooner or later one of the doormen would recognise him anyway and wave him to the front. The night we went to Theatre, the only queue was for the toilet. A man greeted Lars with a hint of poetry – 'Oh, Lars Leese, tall as trees' – and immediately stood aside for him at the urinal. As he did so, he continued to piss, all over the floor.

The little king of Barnsley was also in the disco. Clinton Marcelle leant against the bar, waving us over shyly to join him, and unidentified hands held pints out to us – our 533rd and 534th free drinks, if I'd been counting correctly. Lars was then cornered by someone to talk about the last goal he'd let in, or perhaps about the offside decision that had gone against Barnsley the previous Saturday. I couldn't listen, because Marcelle was too busy asking me how much a Mercedes would cost in Germany. At some point someone in a bright green shirt threw a glass at someone in a bright yellow shirt, fists flew, and we decided it was time to go.

'That was a good evening,' Lars said as we parted on Market Hill. It really had been, but I wasn't sure how much he had enjoyed it himself. He had talked politely to anyone who spoke to him, he had laughed at everyone's jokes, he'd even watched the fist-fight with considerable interest, apparently impressed. But something in his body language suggested to me that he was agitated, as though he was under pressure. 'Sure, when he went out in the evening in Barnsley he was never really himself, because he always felt he was being watched,' Daniela said in retrospect.

However often I sat in cafés or restaurants interviewing professional footballers, I was always startled by the way they clammed up when strangers came to the table and spoke to them. Even players who a minute before – and again a minute later – were giving sharp and intelligent interviews didn't seem quite sure how to respond to strangers. As a last resort, they hid behind a mask of arrogance. Lars didn't have that problem. He talked amicably and patiently to everyone. But even he seemed tense in public.

> You always feel you're being watched. When you pick up your children from nursery school, you think to yourself, 'Are people looking at me in a funny way? Are they angry because we lost?' If you're in the restaurant you think they're looking at your plate to see whether you're eating properly. You can't shake off that thought: 'What effect am I having on these people?' I can imagine that some professionals are really afraid of being approached. Presumably because many of them have had enough bad experiences in the past. You can imagine, if you're playing with Bayern Munich and you're in a restaurant at 11 o'clock in the evening, there'll always be plenty of people who think it's their duty to say, 'What are you doing here at this time of night? I'm calling the coach!' I always liked talking to people in Barnsley, even though I hardly ever made the first move. But I soon found out how hospitable the people there were, whether we had won or lost. Even so, you can never really relax. You're in a nightclub and you know the people in Barnsley think it's cool and normal for footballers to go out for a beer. In England it's all part of it. But you think, 'Hey, I hope no one notices I'm a bit drunk. I hope no one tells the manager I was out till two in the morning.' Basically you always have the stupid feeling of running naked through the town.

By the end of October 1997, the friendliness of the people in Barnsley towards their footballers was being put sorely to the test. They might have clocked up three victories in their first 13 Premiership games, but they had also played a series of matches against the top clubs which had an unfortunate rarity value: 0–5 against Arsenal, 0–6 against Chelsea, 0–7 against Manchester United. 'Our defence was a joke,' complained Danny Wilson after the game in Manchester, 'a suicide squad.' In the *Barnsley Chronicle*, Keith Lodge tried to put things in proportion: 'It isn't all milk and honey in the land of plenty,' he told his readers. But the fans did their best to ignore the run of disastrous defeats. In Manchester, with the score standing at 7–0, they sang, 'We love you Barnsley, we do' so loudly and with such gusto that United's star David Beckham burst out laughing. If they met their players in the town, they went on being polite and cheerful. Until Georgi Hristov opened his mouth.

Of all the international stars Barnsley welcomed, Hristov was the most fêted. At first, hundreds of Hristovs were running through the town: the shirt with number 22 and his name on the back was the best-seller in the supporters' shop. Barnsley had paid Partizan Belgrade a £1.5 million transfer fee for the Macedonian striker; the club had never spent more than £300,000 for a player before then. The papers reported that Hristov had scored a fantastic goal for Macedonia against the Republic of Ireland in a World Cup qualification match. He was ready to be turned into a hero: 'Before every season you look for a player who'll do the job for your team,' said Ian McMillan, 'and ours was Georgi. He would score 20 goals.'

As the autumn drew to a close, he'd scored only two. Hristov seemed to be remote from the rest of the team most of the time, a forlorn figure. Some of his English colleagues treated him as a bit of a joke. Mainly because Hristov – had anyone ever seen the like of it in the dressing-room of an English professional squad? – blow-dried his hair.

Hristov bore the mockery, as he did everything that went on around him, with an equanimity that was astonishing in a 21-year-old – at least he did so outwardly. He radiated an aura of inviolability. What was really going on in his head was a mystery. The only time he smiled was when one of his team-mates made joke about him and everyone laughed heartily. He didn't understand a word of English.

So they had all gone on laughing when the first reports appeared in the tabloids: HRISTOV CLAIMS: 'ENGLISH FOOT-BALLERS DRINK TOO MUCH' It was easy to work out how these quotes might have come about.

'Tell us, Georgi, English footballers drink a lot, don't they?' the reporter would have asked.

'Yes,' Georgi would have replied, and smiled, the way he always did when he didn't understand what was going on.

But this time it was different. This came from an inter view with a Macedonian football magazine. HRISTOV: BARNSLEY GIRLS ARE UGLY was the headline in the *Daily Mirror*, referring to the interview in which the attacker 'had insulted the women of Barnsley in a shocking attack'. They were fat, he claimed, and drank too much beer.

All hell broke loose.

The next day, under the headline GEORGI, LOOK WHAT YOU'VE MISSED!, another newspaper ran a picture of a couple of young beauties from the town.

The club told Hristov not to go into the town centre. The girls of Barnsley might beat him up. 'It was quite seri-ous,' said McMillan. 'Many of us were really disappointed. People felt, how can he come here and then crap on Barnsley like that? That's our women you're talking about!'

How and why an interview in a Macedonian football magazine had made its way to England is a good question. At the time, even English tabloid journalists had started noticing that the many foreign players in the Premier League were much more open in their interviews with reporters from their own countries. It was partly due to the fact that many overseas professionals couldn't express themselves terribly well in English. But the journalists from their home countries were also allies, familiar faces abroad. So some English journalists made a point of going through foreign publications, or even engaging colleagues abroad to pass on the latest footballing gossip. A considerable amount of research must have gone into digging out a Macedonian interview. There was just one problem: Hristov had clearly never said anything like that.

In what we can safely assume were the only phone calls that anyone on the staff of the *Barnsley Chronicle* had ever made to Macedonia, Keith Lodge located the football magazine and had the transcript faxed to him and translated. 'I miss Macedonian women. They are the most beautiful in the world,' read the original text. Put that way, the message seemed to be less of an insult to the women of Barnsley and more of a nostalgic feeling for Macedonia, a state that had just won its independence from Yugoslavia.

Over time, the women of Barnsley came to see the funny side of the story. Georgi Hristov did his penance, and sat on the jury of a beauty competition that was held in the town. Nonetheless, a few weeks later, a woman yelled at Hristov in the town centre: 'Oy, you Macedonian bastard, what do you think of these?' And Hristov stared, in the middle of the street, at a woman with her T-shirt pulled up and her breasts bared.

There are certain rules of conduct for English football teams when they're off the pitch that are passed on from generation to generation. They are supposed to be noisy, to make a nuisance of themselves. Men behaving badly.

In the big clubs like Liverpool or Manchester United, where anything the stars get up to may end up in the papers, this tradition is coming to an end. Dressed in club jackets, in collar and tie, they're usually on their best behaviour when they go on tour. Generally speaking, with the mass arrival of foreign professionals in the mid nineties, the idea was finally dinned into them that a team on the way back from away games doesn't have to drink to the point of oblivion and keel over in a nightclub. But some traditions die slowly. The Dutch midfielder Ruud Gullit, one of the most gifted footballers of the nineties, who played for AC Milan and Chelsea, perhaps sums it up best: 'In an Italian or Dutch dressing-room the players want to have a say about tactics, everyone has his own view to put forward, everyone knows best. In an English dressing-room the players just want to take the piss.'

An English professional team after the end of training could be described, depending on your point of view, as an embarrassing bunch of nursery school children or a mischievous gang of lads. In 1999, a German photographer visited Christian Ziege in Middlesbrough. They were sitting together in the club canteen after the photo-shoot when the photographer suddenly felt a tap on his shoulder. 'Dessert?' someone behind him asked. When he turned round, there stood the incomparable Paul Gascoigne. At hip level, he was holding a plate of fruit out to the photographer. There, among the grapes and bananas, was Gazza's penis.

In the Barnsley dressing-room they held farting competitions: who can fart loudest, who can fart longest?

Once, a German camera crew came to film me in the dressing-room. The other players pelted them with bananas and draped towels over the camera,

and our attacker John Hendrie sang wartime songs. Of course, you sometimes wondered, 'Do they always have to act as though they're in a kindergarten?' At away games we stayed in really decent hotels, four stars and more. And then all of a sudden over dinner someone would start throwing bread rolls at the person sitting opposite him – and then off it went. They fired peas at each other, potatoes went flying through the air. And you had these normal, well-behaved hotel guests sitting right next to us. Often I was a bit ashamed, but when I stole a glance at the people at the next table I saw that they didn't seem at all bothered. And the waiters weren't bothered either. I got the feeling that was the kind of behaviour they more or less expected from a football team.

That was what happened *before* a match; things couldn't really be expected to calm down afterwards. On Saturday nights in Barnsley you could see one footballer or another dancing on top of the juke-box in a bar after downing seven pints. Wearing only his underwear. Treadle's Wine Bar on Peel Parade, a small, badly lit side-street two minutes from Market Hill, was the unofficial meeting-place for Barnsley's professional players on Saturday evenings after a match. In every town or city with a professional club there are certain restaurants or nightclubs that exert a magical attraction on footballers. In many cases they are pseudo-trendy clubs, such as Maximilians in Munich, where people wearing loads of make-up go to meet people with loads of money. Treadle's Wine Bar was Probably the Best Wine Bar in the World. Or at least that's what it said on the waiters' blue shirts. The ceiling was low, the room was bare, plain and undecorated.

There were no chairs or tables. Wine was dispensed from a plastic hose like Coca-Cola or lemonade. But the chief purpose of the wine seemed to be to give the bar its name and a hint of something a bit special. What people generally drank, as they did in the rest of Barnsley, was beer or alcopops. And the music and the clientele were no different from the rest of Barnsley's night-life: cheerful, bare-legged women dancing to mainstream pop songs, cool-looking men in stiffly ironed, bright green shirts nodding their heads in time to the music.

Lars often went there with Swedish defender Peter Markstedt, but they could be sure of bumping into friends there. One player on Barnsley's books could usually be found standing under the steps that led straight to the first floor of the two-storey nightclub.

'It's the best place here, the best place,' he explained to Lars one night, beaming. You got an excellent view from there – up the women's skirts as they climbed the steps.

Women were, of course, the main topic of conversation. At first, Daniela had often gone along to training, as she had done in Leverkusen. 'I thought, if I'm watching, Lars'll make a special effort. That can only be a good thing.' But she soon sensed that she wasn't welcome. Was she imagining it, or were her husband's colleagues really looking at her with irritation, even hostility? 'They couldn't understand that Lars and I were as close as we were, or that I was interested in his training,' she said. 'In their eyes, a woman had no place at the training ground.' So she soon stopped going. But before that happened, she started to understand why it was that some players found a wife at the training ground a bit of a handicap.

There were a couple of girls she'd noticed before. She reckoned they were both about 17, perhaps 18. They watched almost every workout. Once, when Daniela was talking to Lars' friend Peter Markstedt outside the dressing-room, one of the girls came out of the dressing-room block.

'Peter, do you want one too?' she asked. There was still semen hanging from the corner of her mouth.

Markstedt didn't say 'No'. He said 'No, thanks'. As a nation, Swedes tend to be polite.

Given the euphoria surrounding Barnsley's rise to the Premier League it was hardly surprising that football mania spread across the gender divide. It wasn't just traditional supporters who were keen to express their admiration. Now a new breed of female admirer wanted to get as close as possible to the players. Some girls turned it into a curious kind of hunt. Like schoolboys collecting Panini football stickers, they collected sex with professional footballers. Which footballer it was didn't seem to be terribly important. 'The players were like trophies for these girls, and they didn't even notice,' said Daniela.

The trophy-hunt went so far that one evening she was propositioned herself. She was with Vivien Mills, her neighbour and now a friend, in a pub on Wellington Street.

Wasn't she Lars Leese's wife? a young man wanted to know.

'That's right.'

Could he show her that a real Barnsley boy was better in bed than a professional goalkeeper?

'Excuse me?' shouted Daniela. She wasn't sure whether she'd understood correctly. Her English wasn't perfect.

Could he show her that a real Barnsley boy was better in bed than a professional goalkeeper?

'He was quite serious. I don't know if it was a test of courage in front of his mates, or whether he really did think I'd sleep with him. But he was perfectly serious! My friend

Viv laughed her head off, and that helped me to see the funny side. But my eyes almost popped out of my head.'

In Treadle's Wine Bar, meanwhile, her husband was having similarly alarming experiences. There were three of them that night as Peter Markstedt had brought along a friend from Sweden who was visiting. They were standing in a corner when two girls came up to them. They talked a little – at the time everyone in Barnsley, girls included, had an opinion as to why the offside trap hadn't worked the previous Saturday – then one of the girls asked Markstedt's friend if she could borrow his camera for a second.

'What for?' he asked suspiciously.

Don't worry, she wouldn't steal it. Please, could she?

Not wanting to be seen as a coward, the Swede handed it over.

The two girls went to the toilet, and when they came back they handed him his camera.

'So?' asked the Swede.

'Oh, nothing,' said the girls.

It was odd, but it was – as these things often are in bars at night – quickly forgotten.

Three weeks later, Markstedt, who had also moved to Winter Avenue in Royston, went training with Lars. He'd had a call from his friend, Markstedt said. Did Lars remember? His friend had taken the film he had shot in Barnsley to have it developed. The whole thing was filled with pictures of female genitalia.

'That's nothing,' said the Englishmen who had been playing for the club longer then Lars and Markstedt. 'Just you wait for the Christmas party.'

'Listen, son, promise me you'll be careful they don't do anything to you at the Christmas party,' Norman Rimmington had said to Lars – and that was in August. Rimmo, as everyone called him, had worked for Barnsley since 1946, first as a player on a weekly wage of £3, and now, at 73, as the kitman. A likeable man, with bushy white eyebrows and heavy hooded eyelids. When I visit Barnsley in 2001, he's leaning, as ever, against the washing machines that are his empire. He greets me with a firm handshake and tells his stories with paternal authority.

He confesses he felt ashamed in 1997/98 when visiting Premiership teams complained about the dressing-rooms, saying they were far too small and far too hot. The boilers were right above the visitors' dressing-room, and the windows didn't open. 'Colin Todd, Bolton's manager, stood outside the dressing-room with sweat on his forehead and his shirt drenched through. He pointed to my chest with his index finger. "I'm going to report you to the League, you're going to finish us off before the game with these dressing-rooms!"' Rimmo went to Barnsley's chairman John Dennis and told him how embarrassing it was to offer teams like Manchester United dressing-rooms like that. But Dennis just laughed. 'Into the dressing-rooms with them!' he said. 'Let 'em sweat!'

'What times,' Rimmo concludes, 'Barnsley in the Premier League. And the Christmas parties! I always warned Lars: just you be careful at those Christmas parties.'

Norman Rimmington could only guess how Barnsley's footballers celebrated Christmas. The party was for players only, at a secret location. Year after year only hints and rumours reached the outside world about what went on. For those who had been there, one thing was certain: the party was the best, the most fantastic thumping great stonker of a party you could imagine. According to who you spoke to.

Lars knew it was an English tradition to go to a company or club Christmas party in fancy dress. In the Barnsley phonebook he found two companies that supplied costumes. He opted for Bavarian national dress, complete with lederhosen; his friend Peter Markstedt went as a sultan. When they reached the secret location, a remote pub with the sign PRIVATE PARTY on the door, they found Adolf Hitler and a girl in a Heidi costume waiting for them. Striker Neil Thompson had slipped into the role of the Führer; the girl with the blond plaits was the third-choice goalkeeper, Anthony Bullock.

'Heil Hitler!' said Thompson in greeting.

Lars tried to laugh.

'If you walked around like that in Germany you'd be arrested within ten minutes,' he said.

'How come?' asked Thompson irritably.

And all the old prejudices were confirmed. The Germans have no sense of humour, thought Thompson. And not all Englishmen have one, thought Lars.

But any animosities quickly faded. It was three o'clock in the afternoon, and the party began. The plan was to get drunk as quickly as possible.

Practically from the first day of training in July I was forever hearing, 'Just you wait till the Christmas party, ho ho.' And that stuff about fancy dress sounded good, too. Although I was completely bowled over when I went to the costume hire shop – all the Nazi uniforms hanging up in there. On the day of the Christmas party some of the men even came to training in fancy dress. Ashley Ward was the Pink Panther, someone else was a dragon, John Hendrie was wearing a purple suit. He was a Scouser, he said; the people of Liverpool had a reputation for thieving. When I saw Hitler and the Nazi girl, I thought, 'Oh

Christ.' But it was OK. And then there was just drinking after that. Fifty men – the reserve team and the
youth team were there as well – at three o'clock in
the afternoon in an empty pub. Bottoms up! At some
point all of a sudden a great shout went up and two
strippers came in. The youth players had to help
them get undressed, and when the two women were
naked, two players jumped on to the stage and had
sex with them. In front of the whole team. Football's
a macho world. On Monday morning in our dressing-room, you could have rewritten the *Guinness Book
of Records*: they were all the greatest, they had all
drunk 125 beers and slept with 99 women. But the
Christmas party, I don't know, that was – well, I'd
have to say it was what you might call an acquired
taste. Specially the fact that so much fuss was made
of it. I think we could all have gone out on a quite
normal Saturday in Barnsley and had more fun.

A few days later there was another Christmas party, the
club's official do for all its staff. The players brought their wives
or girlfriends with them, and everyone sat together over dinner
in the banqueting room of the Ardsley House Hotel. Candles
on the table. Friendly small-talk. Then, when a few women
suggested going dancing in town, the footballers sighed with
regret. Oh, they were so tired. A nightclub, at this time of
night? You've got to be joking.
On their best behaviour, all of a sudden.

8

YOU'LL NEVER WALK ALONE

A T FIVE TO three a bell rang in the depths of Anfield. In the visitors' dressing-room a few Barnsley players plucked at their shirts, just to keep their hands busy. 'Off we go, lads!' said team captain Neil Redfearn. Just to say something. The bell kept on jangling. In the Bundesliga, the referee gives a good blast on his whistle five minutes before kick-off as a signal to the players to get out of the dressing-room. In the Premier League, an electric bell rings, as loud and insistent as a school bell at the beginning of class.

The piercing din of the bell on 22 November at Anfield alarmed Lars Leese, but at the same time he found it re-assuring. Top sportsmen often go through moments like that shortly before the start of play. All of a sudden the tension eases, the nerves vanish, and for a moment they feel deep calm and security. That moment rarely lasts for long.

Lars hadn't played for seven weeks. Only at the team meeting an hour and a half before the start of the match had he learned that manager Danny Wilson was changing goalkeeper once again. He had been hoping he would play since final training on Friday, when Wilson had put him with the first eleven. But *knowing* you're going to play is different from hoping. It greatly increases the joy, the fear and, above all, the pressure.

For the Liverpool game, Wilson had dropped five players from the previous line-up, which had lost 4–1 to Southampton. 'Why can't our goalkeeper save one like that?' Wilson had shouted in desperation in Southampton when their keeper Paul Jones made a spectacular save and David Watson let in a goal just a few seconds later. There was nothing Watson could have done, but there was no point going to the manager to tell him that. He had had enough.

Barnsley had had enough, too. The fans and, up to a point, the players had enjoyed their image of being cheerful losers. It was great to hear on television what a loveable club Barnsley was, to read in the paper how much fun the fans were, still singing their heads off in Manchester even when they were losing 7–0. But of course part of the reason the fans had been singing so cheerfully was that they thought things would get better the following Saturday. Only a few people still believed that after their defeat in Southampton. Barnsley were at the bottom of the Premiership and, much worse than that, they were disillusioned. The honeymoon was over.

In the *Barnsley Chronicle*, K. K. Lomax of Wordsley in the West Midlands wrote an open letter to the team: 'I have many friends who follow Aston Villa. It gives me no pleasure to inform you that in the eyes of the fans at Villa Park, you are the joke team in the Premier League. There is a huge and increasing delight at the "Laurel and Hardy antics" of the shower at Oakwell. I know that you can stay up. Alternatively you can go straight back down as the clowns who should never have had the audacity to come up in the first place!' The words three columns to the left weren't much more encouraging. 'When players put on a Barnsley shirt, they should want to die for the club. I was hurt more than I can say last Saturday when there was such an obvious lack of commitment, not just from one or two of them, but from the entire team, from back to front. They are accepting defeat too easily, almost as if it doesn't matter to them.' The words were Danny Wilson's.

Just so that absolutely everyone understood how serious things were, the manager put the team up in a hotel in Liverpool the night before the match. In Serie A or the Bundesliga that would be perfectly normal practice. Teams should be in hotels before a match. In England, and above all where Barnsley were concerned, it was unusual. For home games, the squad met at the stadium an hour and a half before kick-off, and at away games within a radius of 100 miles, like the Liverpool match, they would normally take the bus on Saturday morning and stop somewhere along the route for a spot of lunch. Everyone could order his favourite meal. Lars always had spaghetti bolognese; many English players ordered beans on toast. On one occasion captain Neil Redfearn brought his own lunchbag, from McDonald's.

Though professional football became an international affair in the late nineties, when at almost every level teams played with five or more foreigners, some traditions were stubbornly maintained which justified people talking about English or Spanish football as though they were different worlds. What Wilson did on Friday evening, when they arrived at their hotel in Liverpool, was English football; he took the team to a pub. But only to drink a beer or two, just to help them sleep better.

Clack, clack! went the studs of their boots as the footballers marched across the concrete floor. At most stadiums the tunnel from the dressing-room to the pitch isn't longer than

30 feet; at Anfield it's about 30 yards long. At the end it goes up two steps, then passes through a narrow exit. When the players went down the tunnel, they couldn't see much of what was ahead of them. They could only hear the stadium. The noise increased with each step they took.

> *When you walk through a storm*
> *Hold your head up high*
> *And don't be afraid of the dark.*
> *At the end of a storm*
> *There's a golden sky*
> *And the sweet, silver song of a lark.*
> *Walk on through the wind,*
> *Walk on through the rain,*
> *Though your dreams be tossed and blown.*
> *Walk on, walk on with hope in your heart,*
> *And you'll never walk alone!*
> *You'll never walk alone.*

At least 30,000 of the 41,000 spectators that made up the crowd that day were singing the Liverpool anthem. Of course, when Richard Rodgers and Oscar Hammerstein wrote the song in 1945 for the sentimental Broadway musical *Carousel*, they hadn't had in mind a beer-fuelled open-air male-voice choir. You'll never walk alone. But of course the song made Liverpool's opponents feel that that was precisely what they were doing; once they heard the great wall of sound from the terraces, they *were* walking alone. Hearing 30,000 people singing a song, a proper song, is a rare and gripping experience. Every time I sat in the stands at Anfield Road and heard them singing, I was thrown into emotional confusion. The song was so touching, but at the same time so powerful, that I was afraid it was going to crush me. And I was only *writing* about the match. What must it be like for the boys who have to go out there on the pitch? How many matches have been lost in that long, narrow tunnel, before the game has even begun? How many teams have been intimidated by this song, forcing its way through the tunnel walls and into their very bone marrow? How many visitors have been overwhelmed by the aura surrounding the 18-times League champions and four-times European Cup winners, Liverpool FC?

At the end of the tunnel, where the players have only two steps left to climb before they find themselves in the eye of the storm, there is a sign: THIS IS ANFIELD. The Liverpool players touch it with their right hand; it's supposed to bring them luck. Lars read it with a lump in his throat.

He was right at the front. Traditionally, the goalkeeper is the second man, after the captain, to come out of the tunnel. When he had been warming up 45 minutes earlier, the Anfield stands had still been empty and the only noise came from the PA system. Ever since British stadiums were turned into seated arenas in the early nineties, the spectators have arrived at the very last minute. Their seat is guaranteed; they don't have to fight for a good view as they had to in the days of terraces. After his warm-up, Lars had gone back to the dressing-room to change his kit again. There, he had felt the stadium filling up. Every few minutes the door opened as the players came back from warming up, and each time the chants of 'Liverpool, Liverpool!' echoed louder around the dressing-room. But nothing had prepared them for the singing at three minutes to three: Walk on, walk on, with hope in your heart! Thirty thousand voices practically carried Lars on to the pitch. It was scary and enjoyable at the same time. It was Anfield.

In 1997, Liverpool didn't have anything like an outstanding

team. It was seven years since they had won their last championship. However passionately, however desperately Liverpool tried to bring back the successes of the seventies and eighties, the only thing the team had won in recent years was a new nickname – the Spice Boys. Players like David James, Steve McManaman and Robbie Fowler were 'more interested in fashion shows, fast cars and nice hairstyles than hard work', claimed the *Guardian*, and that was how they played. Liverpool's feline passing was wonderful to behold, but there was no real power behind it.

Liverpool had won fewer than half of their first 13 games in the 1997/98 Premier League season and the team was battling to stay up with the leaders. But as far as Lars was concerned, the club and the stadium had lost little of their fascination. Born in 1969, he belonged to a generation whose childhood had coincided with Liverpool's best years. That kind of thing stays with you. To anyone who was first allowed to stay up past ten o'clock at the age of seven or eight to watch the European Cup highlights on television with their dad, Liverpool isn't just a name, it's a myth. It was the time when 'the boys in red' made the European Cup their domain. Kenny Dalglish, Kevin Keegan, Graeme Souness. Even today, the names of the Liverpool players are synonymous with greatness.

The glorious past is always with us. The programme for the Barnsley game reminded the crowd that another three goals would take Liverpool to 4,000 goals in League matches at Anfield. Who could doubt that they would get those goals against Barnsley?

Only five minutes in, Lars brought the crowd to its feet for the first time. Nicky Eaden, Barnsley's right-back, passed the ball back to Lars and he attempted to control it – badly. The ball was too close to him, and Lars found himself too cramped to kick it upfield with any power. And Karlheinz Riedle,

Liverpool's German striker, much-loved at Anfield for his tireless dedication, was steaming towards him. Lars tried to move the ball a bit to the left, but Riedle had anticipated the manoeuvre and put himself between the goalkeeper and the ball. It was a nightmare: just five minutes into the game, his first contact with the ball, a common-or-garden back-pass, and he'd let in Liverpool for their opening goal. At least it should have been. In desperation, Lars threw himself into a last-ditch tackle; as though Riedle were growing a third leg, Lars' left foot shot out from behind him. Had he touched Riedle, it would almost certainly have been a penalty, but Lars just managed to get hold of the ball. He walloped it over the touchline. The Liverpool fans shouted, 'Dodgy keeper! Dodgy keeper!'

Nothing had happened, I tried to persuade myself. Just get rid of the ball and get on with things. But it wasn't as easy as that. With every back-pass I heard a dissatisfied rumble behind my goal – the worried murmur of the Barnsley fans and the hopeful curses of the Liverpool supporters. An experienced goalkeeper would probably just have ignored the spectators, but I was too much of a fan myself. I listened to their songs, I listened to them grumbling, and I found myself wondering – right in the middle of the game – what are the Barnsley fans saying about you right now? Hey, concentrate on the game I had to tell myself. Perhaps I'd have done things differently, taken better control of the situation, if I'd completely blanked out the fans. On the other hand, I'm glad I absorbed the atmosphere in the stadium the way I did. I can remember another game, the 3–0 defeat against Aston Villa. Princess Diana had died six days before, so there was a minute's silence before the match. The players stood

in a semi-circle, the referee blew the whistle for the minute's silence, and all of a sudden Oakwell, filled with 18,000 people, went completely quiet. Absolutely silent. Two birds flew over the stadium, and you could hear their wing-beats. That's how quiet it was. I listened to the silence in fascination. Then, when the minute was up, the stadium exploded. We switched immediately from absolute silence to an absolutely deafening din, as though someone had turned a dial from nought to a hundred. Perhaps I'd have performed better if I'd concentrated on the coming game during that minute's silence, rather than thinking about the wing-beats of those birds. There's no way of knowing. Today, at any rate, I'm glad I have those memories: the intensity of that one-minute silence. The grumbling of the fans after my collision with Riedle. The perfect goalkeeper is one who spends the whole game in a tunnel, blanks out everything going on around him. If he really exists, I admire him – and I feel sorry for him. When his career's over, and people ask him what it's like to play in front of 41,000 people, he'll have to say, 'I don't know, I never noticed.' He'll be missing something.

Fifteen minutes into the game, Liverpool's Czech midfielder Patrick Berger had a high, whistling shot on goal from about 30 yards out. It was fierce, cunningly struck and spinning furiously. Flutter-ball, footballers call it. It wobbled through the air, and it wasn't until it was right in front of Lars that he was sure exactly where it was headed. Lars flew to the right and stopped the shot with both hands, mouth wide open. He didn't hear the roar of acknowledgement behind his goal. He was too busy catching the ball.

At home in Barnsley, the poet sat by his radio. Like many others, he hadn't been able to get hold of a ticket for Anfield, Liverpool having released only 1,900 tickets for the visiting fans. The fact that the game was being broadcast on the radio made the afternoon rather more bearable, though. Sometimes, Ian McMillan followed away games on Teletext. He would stare at the mute television screen and wait for the score to change. 'I must be mad,' he later acknowledged, but now, as he sat by the radio, he wasn't so sure. Perhaps it was better on Teletext after all. 'The radio report was torture. Barnsley were trapped in their own half, just defending. And of course the commentator wasn't saying, "A shot from Berger – no, it's OK, Leese has it covered." No, the commentator, that hellhound, screamed, "A shot from Berger, dangerous . . ." and then he'd drag out the agony before, finally, ". . . saved by Leese." In that breath before the all-clear I'd died a hundred deaths.'

After 30 minutes of play there was still no reason for Barnsley supporters to turn off the radio. Given their disastrous performances against the other top clubs things were going better than might have been expected. True, Barnsley were seeing less and less of the ball, but the team was defending with great intensity and a considerable amount of skill – and the game was still scoreless. Danny Wilson had given Adrian Moses the task of following Liverpool's serpentine dribbler McManaman wherever he went. That kind of man-marking is despised at the top end of modern football, where it's considered a bit Stalinist, but Wilson could no longer afford to take such opinions into account. Moses did an excellent job. Whenever McManaman got the ball, Moses blocked his route to goal. He forced the snake-man out on to the wing, where his dribbling was useless, because McManaman isn't a great crosser of the ball.

Liverpool went on attacking. Lars caught one corner in mid-air and suddenly stumbled, lost his balance and fell to the ground. Unseen by the referee, Riedle had given him a bit of a shove. He stood innocently right next to Lars and waited for the off-balance goalkeeper to let the ball slip out of his hands. Lars clung on to it for dear life.

Barnsley allowed themselves to be forced further and further into their own half. Only very occasionally did they break out. Andy Liddell, nominally an attacker but a de facto defensive midfielder, risked advancing into Liverpool's penalty area every now and then, but most of the Barnsley players were stuck behind the halfway line, so his options were limited. All of a sudden, Liverpool's goalkeeper David James came running at him.

James had an unusually daring interpretation of the goal-keeper's role. He was practically a sweeper, he acted offensively, he played further out of goal than keepers tend to. On most days he was among the best in the Premier League. Unfortunately when he made a mistake, he had a knack of looking really stupid. Calamity James, they called him in the tabloids. Only he can tell you why he ran out off his line like that; he might not even know himself. Liddell was on the far right of the penalty area, and from there he was no real threat to Liverpool's goal. When James came charging at him, Liddell had a go, but without any great hope. His honour as a striker decreed that he shot whenever a goalkeeper was storming at him. James saved, but he couldn't hold on to the ball. It came within Liddell's reach again, but he was in such an unfavourable position that he could only belt it inelegantly towards the middle of the penalty area. Patrick Berger was tracking back for Liverpool, only to demonstrate that fine attackers like him have no business playing in defence. The ball bounced wildly off his shin, straight to the feet of Barnsley's goal-poacher

Ashley Ward. Before the ping-pong game between friend and foe could become any more ludicrous, Ward hustled the ball into the net. After 35 minutes Barnsley were leading Liverpool by a goal to nil. For the first and only time that afternoon, Barnsley's defenders appeared in their opponents' half, and that was just to congratulate Ward.

Ian McMillan devoted one of his poems to that moment. The last four lines went:

> *Ward scored!*
> *Ward scored!*
> *Ward scored!*
> *(repeat until exhausted)*

Now the fun really began. Ward's goal was like the moment in bullfighting when the bull sees the red rag. Except that Liverpool refused to lower their heads and run blindly, horns straight out ahead of them, at Barnsley's goal. They camped in Barnsley's half and stubbornly continued their elegant passing game. It was good to see Jamie Redknapp, Patrick Berger and Öyvind Leonhardsen working together. The ball ran back and forth, back and across. But Liverpool kept running out of space, as nine Barnsley players worked hard to close them down. The minute one of the defenders got the ball, he hoofed it forwards as hard as he could, and Ashley Ward, the lone man up front, ran after it, generally to no great effect. The Barnsley fans cheered every time anyway, as though a goal had been scored. If the ball was in Liverpool's half, then at least they didn't have to worry about their opponents scoring in the next three seconds. That was generally how long it took before a Liverpool defender passed the ball back into midfield and the siege began all over again.

Karlheinz Riedle, who kept slipping his marker with ease only to fluff every chance he created, was suddenly alone in front of Lars. This time he did everything right by trying to put the ball between his compatriot's legs, but Lars pulled his legs together and saved. Minutes later Lars saved again: a one-on-one with Leonhardsen. Sitting in the press-box it seemed to Keith Lodge, the reporter from the *Barnsley Chronicle*, that things were running an inevitable course. 'Only Liverpool were playing now, and the pressure was getting unbearable. But whatever they did, Lars' hands, feet and whatever other body parts were in the way. When he saved again in the middle of the second half, I was suddenly quite certain: they're not going to score. Because we all know those games. One team keeps on storming, while the other team has only one chance at goal and wins.'

On the pitch, Lars had the same sense. He stood in the eye of the storm and started to feel good. When he fetched a ball from behind the goal-line, he walked deliberately along behind the goal, right past the Liverpool fans. 'Let one in, you fucking bastard!' they shouted. Lars smiled at them.

The way I played with the fans was pretty coarse and provocative. I should never have allowed myself to be distracted like that. But I'd saved so many shots that I felt unbeatable. 'Come on! Come on!' I said to myself as Liverpool's attacks rolled on. And all of a sudden, although nothing particular had happened, my feelings completely changed ten minutes before the end of the game. We can't possibly be winning here, Barnsley in Liverpool, I thought all of a sudden. Surely something stupid's going to happen to us. For heaven's sake, just be sure you're not the one who fucks up. Then I calmed myself down with the thought: a 1–1

draw would still be a good result. Don't worry about letting a goal in, Lars, you're allowed one mistake.

Ian McMillan didn't want to be there in case it happened. He left his radio. 'Tell me when it's over,' he said to his daughter before locking himself in the lavatory. There he sat, trousers on, on the toilet, waiting for the minutes to pass at Anfield.

The fans were still urging Liverpool ever onwards. In many stadiums the crowd derives some satisfaction from getting on their own team's backs when things are going wrong. In Liverpool, they saved that option for the final whistle; over 30,000 people were still trying to roar the ball into the net. Midfielder Danny Murphy came on for defender Stig Björnebye, because why did Liverpool need any defenders? Murphy immediately fired off a lightning shot, 25 yards from the goal. When Lars went to catch the ball, the weight of the shot sprained his wrist. The pain would stay with him for weeks. But at least he had the ball. Barnsley defender Arjan de Zeeuw turned to his goalkeeper and clenched his fist. Lars understood. It meant: give everything you can.

Lars sent another goal-kick deep into the Liverpool half. And then Ian McMillan's daughter let him out of the toilet. It was over. Barnsley had won in Liverpool, 1–0 at Anfield. Lars turned around and enthusiastically grabbed his bottle of water out of the net. That was his first reaction after every game; he instinctively performed that ordinary gesture even at the moment of his greatest triumph. The spectators behind him were applauding Lars and they were Liverpool fans. The Barnsley fans were sitting at the other end of the stadium. Lars took one last leap in their direction. As he jumped, he raised his fists in the air, his face contorted with joy, his mouth and eyes agape, celebration etched right across his face. In the coming days he could look at himself as often as he wanted to: the newspapers had captured the moment in a photograph. And every time he saw the picture he thought he could hear the fans shouting again: 'Lars Leece! Lars Leece!' Lars grabbed defender Nicky Eaden in front of the supporters' end, but Eaden pushed the German away. He was too exhausted to celebrate.

I wanted to do the works – parties, fiestas, a carnival in Liverpool. But the other players crept back to the dressing-room, heads hanging. They were that wiped out. The only one who came up to me was a steward. 'Calm down,' he said, 'or you'll drive the Barnsley fans completely wild.' So I went to the dressing-room as well. There were only dead men sitting there. I went up to each of them. 'Hey, hey, we won at Anfield!' but they only groaned, 'Leave me alone.' That was the difference: as a goalkeeper you're mentally exhausted but physically fresh; the other players were physically finished. Being the prince of the carnival all on your own isn't a lot of fun, so I sat down on the bench beside them, rested my head in my hands and tried to enjoy my delight in peace. But quite honestly that isn't my thing. I wanted to explode with joy. When we were on our way out of the stadium, some Liverpool fans smashed our windscreen with a brick, and I wanted to get out of the bus and chase after them. 'You'll stay right here!' said the manager. I was completely wound up.

Had anyone in Barnsley lost faith in the team before the Liverpool game? You'd have to be joking. People had always said the lads needed a bit of time to get used to the bracing winds of the Premier League. All they needed was a catalyst, a victory like the one they'd now got in Liverpool. Barnsley were really going to get going. They were on the way up now; one off the bottom. That's the kind of thing people in Barnsley said after their 1–0 victory. And they really believed it.

How easy it was to get up on Sunday morning. Lars went to a number of different shops; it would have been too embarrassing for him to buy all the papers in the same newsagent's. The *News of the World* had him in their team of the day; the *Sunday Times* said Lars had enjoyed 'a happy life in Barnsley's goal'; 'They were all heroes, from the impressive Leese to striker Andy Liddell, who ran and ran,' wrote the *Mirror*. Very touched, but also slightly baffled, Lars said to himself, 'I wasn't *that* good.' But that wasn't what people wanted to hear. The *Deutsche Presse Agentur* phoned up, and Germany's football fans, most of whom had no idea where Barnsley was or who Lars Leese was, were told by the goalkeeper in a lengthy article: 'When we came back from Liverpool, the people celebrated the way they did in 1966 when England won the World Cup.'

The DJ in the Theatre on Wellington Street turned the music off when Lars and a few colleagues came into the club that Saturday evening. 'A big hello to the heroes of Anfield!' yelled the DJ. A few young men in ironed neon blue or bright green shirts with too much gel in their hair hoisted Lars on to their shoulders. For a moment, the club didn't need any music. The people were singing: 'Walk on, walk on, with hope in your heart, and you'll never walk alone. You'll never walk alone . . .'

Later, Lars Leese walked alone, quickly. He was walking home. Too drunk with all the free beer, too intoxicated with joy.

9

THE DODGY CHICKEN

LIVERPOOL MADE LARS Leese famous. The Premiere television channel came all the way from Hamburg to interview him; Darton High School, a few miles outside Barnsley, invited him to give them a German lesson; and at his first home game after his triumph at Anfield, even the supporters of the opposing team were keen to greet him. Dozens of the 2,500 Leeds United fans stretched out their right arms in a Hitler salute and shouted 'Sieg Heil!'

Showing no outward emotion, Lars walked towards where the Leeds fans sat drenched in the rain and went to work. But inside he was shivering. He was flabbergasted. Nothing had prepared him for such an encounter – the Christmas party with the Hitler look-alike and the Heidi girl with the plaits was still a few weeks off.

Thinking about it later, Lars remembered a conversation he'd had with Barnsley striker Andy Liddell after the League Cup match against Chesterfield in September.

'How can you stand the fans yelling at you like that?' Liddell asked him.

'Yelling?'

'You know, the Chesterfield supporters behind your goal.'

'I didn't hear anything.'

'You didn't? OK, fine.'

After the Leeds game, Lars began to grasp what Liddell might have been talking about.

It's a fact that when many Englishmen see a German they immediately think of war and football; the two events are somehow mixed up together. 'Stand up if you won the war!' sang English fans during the World Cup qualifier in September 2001 in Munich. In 1996, when the Goethe Institute in London asked English schoolchildren between the ages of 14 and 16 to list the ten most famous Germans, some pupils mentioned 'Helmit Coal' or 'Hermit Kolle'. Even when this had been adjusted to Helmut Kohl, the former chancellor lagged hopelessly behind. The ones who made it into the top ten were six sportsmen, three Nazis and Ludwig van Beethoven. The clear winner, and thus the most famous German of all, was the Austrian Adolf Hitler, with 68 per cent, ahead of the then captain of the national football team Jürgen Klinsmann with 47 per cent. Kohl himself was pipped by Hermann Göring.

For a German like Lars Leese, who had been brought up with an awareness that you talked about the Second World War with care and tact if you talked about it at all, the English obsession with the war was confusing. What did it have to do with football, and how on earth could the English go around making jokes about it?

In his book *Four Two*, devoted to the English World Cup victory over Germany in 1966, David Thomson wrote that the English saw the match as an extension of the war. More than thirty-five years later, little has changed. The English were on the winning side in both world wars, and they are proud of that, because they were fighting on the side of good. So they see war as something just, something the Germans can safely be reminded of, particularly if one comes up against them in a soccer match. On one of my trips to Middlesbrough's training ground I ran into the legendary Paul Gascoigne. He did not, as he had done to that German photographer, offer me his penis in a plate of fruit, but he did greet me enthusiastically with the words, 'Another German – do I have to talk about the fucking war again?'

As far as the English public were concerned, it was the Liverpool game that turned Lars Leese into a German. Before then, outside Barnsley few people knew anything much about him. It was only when the reports came in from Anfield that anyone noticed they had a German in goal. After Liverpool, in the eyes of the opposing supporters, Lars Leese was suddenly worthy of note. He was the enemy in more ways than one.

The provocative chants and gestures in the stadium were bearable, though. The only actual attacks by fans came in the playground of Darton High School after Lars' German lesson. Thirteen-year-old girls grabbed his bottom while he was signing autographs.

As far as Danny Wilson was concerned, the goalkeeper question was resolved by that match at Anfield. 'By the time we were driving home from Liverpool, I'd made my decision,' he said. 'Lars was going to be my number one for the rest of the season.' Seven days later, at home against Leeds, he would not regret his decision. The rain in Yorkshire was so torrential that you can see it in photographs of the match, but on that one occasion the spectators in Barnsley could actually make believe they were in Rio. 'It's just like watching Brazil,' 18,000 people chanted through the downpour.

The Times discovered a 'samba rhythm' in Barnsley's unexpectedly confident exchanges. Captain Redfearn played one quality pass after another, and by the half-hour mark Andy Liddell and Ashley Ward had given their team, second from bottom in the table, a two-goal lead over the team fourth from the top. With two breathtakingly skilful saves, Lars repelled shots first from Rod Wallace and later from Jimmy Floyd Hasselbaink. It was Barnsley's best game of the season so far. After 90 minutes they had lost 3–2. Two goals from Leeds in the last ten minutes had turned the match on its head. 'Defeat's a bit like death,' Lars told journalists.

Nine days later they lost 2–1 to Sheffield Wednesday, Wednesday's winner coming in the 88th minute. That was followed by a 2–2 draw against Newcastle United that didn't really please anyone. Once again, Barnsley were bottom of the Premiership – but they still felt good. 'No one can point a finger at our lads,' declared Danny Wilson. Bad results? 'Good performances,' countered the manager.

The team had its photograph taken, smiling cheerfully, for the programme, with the players wearing both their red shirts and a Father Christmas hat with a gold bell on the end. SANTA IS A BARNSLEY FAN read the inscription on the hats. The Christmas cards began to stack up on the dressing-room benches.

In Great Britain, unlike in Germany, passing on Christmas greetings to your colleagues, formally and in writing, is taken extremely seriously, even if you spend the rest of the year communicating chiefly in farts and insults. Lars, who didn't know about this tradition, was initially bewildered when the first cards landed on his seat, deposited there without further comment by players who were changing just six feet away. But he quickly realised that he ought to get hold of some cards as well. Shortly before Christmas, every Barnsley player had written to all the others, and each one had thanked all the others for their Christmas cards. And they weren't even going to be apart for the Christmas holidays. While most European leagues take a week-long winter break, in Great Britain an unusually large number of games are played over Christmas. Football is traditionally a part of the festive season. Barnsley had to play on 20, 26 and 28 December, and then again on 3 January. 'We had a weird sort of Christmas with our families, between training and the matches,' said the Norwegian striker Jan Aage Fjörtoft. Lars thought the timetable was some kind of joke. But Fjörtoft had been playing in England for more than four years and had long since grown accustomed to the Christmas sporting season. 'You have so many games in this country, after a few years you don't even notice it's Christmas, and you forget all about New Year,' he said. The previous year, for example, Fjörtoft had had to play Arsenal with his club at the time, Middlesbrough. 'We spent New Year's Eve in a filthy London hotel. We were in bed long before midnight, as we would have been for any other game – it was all completely normal. And the next day we lost. Playing for Middlesbrough, that was normal as well.'

The myth lives on that there's something special about bank holiday matches. It was on Christmas Day 1935 that Tranmere Rovers defeated Oldham 13–4; it was on Christmas Day 1963 that Fulham beat Ipswich Town 10–1. The club history observed: 'Fulham played as if they had some sort of sly murder in mind.' In the past, there have always been curious results over Christmas, claimed Gordon Pallister, who captained Barnsley after the Second World War. 'That unusual atmosphere must have inspired the players,' he explained to me. 'I mean, all those spectators, not all that booze.'

Pallister turned 80 in 1997, but whenever he went along

to Oakwell a few people would always recognise him and call out, 'Hey, Gordon, are you playing today?' And Pallister would beam. It didn't take much to make him happy – he was completely at peace with himself. 'Christmas,' he sighed as we sank into deep leather chairs at his home. On Boxing Day in 1946, Barnsley had drawn 4–4 with Southampton. 'What a result, what a game,' said Pallister. 'I always played well in Southampton. They could have blindfolded me and my passes would have hit the mark. In those days we had a striker called Cecil McCormack. He was like that German who could hit the goal from anywhere at all – what's his name?'

'Gerd Müller?'

'Gird Mooler, yes. Our Cecil. He'd drink three scotches before a game, and then score.'

'So alcohol really was responsible for those legendary Christmas results?'

'No' said Pallister. 'McCormack always drank three scotches, before every match.'

In Pallister's day, three games in four days over Christmas was considered perfectly normal. With doctors and coaches now complaining that playing so many games without a proper chance to recover is ruining the health of professional footballers, the number of bank holiday games has dwindled, but for tradition's sake there will be at least a full Premier League programme on Boxing Day for a long time to come. On 26 December 1997 Barnsley were due to play in Bolton. The stadium would be sold out, the terraces red because most of the crowd would be wearing Santa hats. Whenever a goal was scored they would sing Christmas carols. 'Look forward to it,' Lars' team-mates told him.

Before then, however, on 20 December, Barnsley had to survive an away game against Tottenham Hotspur.

Three days earlier Lars had become a father for the second time. His son Christopher was born in Barnsley General Hospital. Andy Mills, the Leeses' friend and neighbour from Winter Avenue, saw them as a perfect happy family: 'Lars was number one at the club, Daniela was less shy and starting to feel at ease, and her little daughter used to go marching around the whole estate, just walking into neighbours' houses whenever she felt like it. I had a sense that if Barnsley had offered Lars a 59-year contract he and Daniela would immediately have agreed to it.'

The game in north London really began four or five days before kick-off. As so often happens in the week before a big match, if there's no actual news the media go over and over the game for days beforehand. Barnsley were bottom of the table with 14 points, Tottenham third from bottom with 16 points. Although they still had half a season ahead of them, most of the people involved were getting increasingly worked up, convinced that the game would decide the fate of the two clubs. Barnsley, the nation's favourite outsider, would take on Tottenham, who despite the fact that they hadn't won a championship since 1961 still thought of themselves as a great club, and hurl them into the abyss. That was the scenario. Over the past few weeks Barnsley had been encouraging on the field, although they hadn't gained much in the way of points; during the same period Tottenham had lost 6–1 to Chelsea and 4–0 to Coventry. In a poem penned for this match, Ian McMillan wrote:

> We must be tighter at the back
> than my grandma's corset.
> We must be sharper at the front
> than my grandma's bra . . .

The *Daily Express*, by its own estimation a 'quality tabloid' – whatever that might be – reproduced a version of Tottenham's emblem, the cockerel perched proudly on the ball swapped for a Christmas turkey under the headline BARNSLEY BOSS WILSON PROMISES: 'WE'RE GOING TO STUFF YOU!' In the accompanying text there was no quotation that might have justified the headline – understandably enough, because an honourable man like Wilson would never have said anything disparaging about other teams. But in the fever ish atmosphere before the big match few people cared whether the article actually referred to the quote in the headline. The main thing was that the headline sounded good.

It was the fashion that month to laugh at Tottenham. To a certain extent Spurs and its fans had brought it on themselves; they couldn't stop harking on about the glory days and what a big club Tottenham was. It was time for them to have a look at the table. Added to this was the fact that the Spurs manager was an easy target for mockery and malice. Spurs' chairman Alan Sugar had presented the new manager, the Swiss coach Christian Gross, as a kind of saviour, despite the fact that hardly anyone in England had heard of him. That wasn't necessarily Gross's fault: he had a good record with Grasshopper Zurich in Switzerland, so the fact that no one knew who he was said more about the ignorance of English football than it did about anything else. But the unfortunate Gross fed their prejudices with some embarrassingly cack-handed gestures. At his first press conference at White Hart Lane he suddenly took a pink ticket out of his jacket pocket. 'Here, I show you my ticket,' he announced in broken English. His initiative was an interesting one: he had used the underground to get from the airport to the stadium to show how close he was to the Tottenham fans

– he took the tube, just as they did. Unfortunately his English was not good enough to sell the idea convincingly to the dozens of journalists present. When Gross, still holding his tube ticket aloft, had finished his confused explanation, a journalist asked him, all friendly concern, 'So you've been having problems with public transport?'

The match against Barnsley would be the day of judgement – for both clubs.

For Lars Leese the game was just as important as it was for everyone else in Barnsley, although for a slightly different reason: it was the first game he'd played in to be broadcast in Germany. ARD were going to show lengthy highlights in their Sunday *Sportschau* programme. Reporter Thorsten Winkler came to Barnsley to film two days beforehand, and explained to Lars that they were going to put an extra camera behind the goal just to follow him during the game.

It was a bright December day, and the stadium, with 28,000 excited fans, was sold out. And after 17 minutes it was all over. Or rather, the duel that everyone was so keenly anticipating never took place. As though paralysed, Barnsley let their opponents do whatever they liked. Spurs' Darren Anderton passed to Allan Nielsen, who was standing unattended on the edge of the penalty box. He had the time and space to trap the ball, look around, turn, and strike an unhurried shot past Lars without even raising a sweat. And that was only five minutes in. Seven minutes later Nielsen headed to David Ginola, who was being covered by the three Barnsley defenders. None of them picked him up, though, and he had time to get a low shot in. It didn't look particularly dangerous but somehow the ball slipped under Lars' body and into the goal. Lars stood up slowly and pointed furiously with his right hand – which, in its white goalkeeper's glove, looked enormous – at the spot where Ginola had been able to stand unmarked. It was a desperate reflex; Lars knew he should really have been pointing that index finger at himself. It was only another five minutes before Ginola, unmarked in the penalty area again, made the score 3–0 with a header. Behind the goal, ARD man Winkler 'had almost fainted. Of course, you're a journalist, and you should n't care how the guy you're reporting on is playing. But at that moment I felt nothing but pity for Leese.'

From 40 yards away, you could tell how the goalkeeper was suffering. In the second half he fired a series of goal-kicks over the touchline or straight to Tottenham players. After one particularly hopeless clearance he cursed loudly to himself. That amounted to a capitulation. The rule in sport is that once you've displayed your nerves, you're lost. From the purely factual point of view, Lars didn't do badly after Spurs scored for the third time. There were no further goals after the 17th minute, he caught a few crosses in a busy penalty area, and he saved a few shots. But the *effect* on the spectators was as though the next collapse was only a matter of minutes away. His body language betrayed him: his harried expression, his hectic lunges at the ball, the panicky rebounds. The press-box at White Hart Lane is right by the edge of the pitch, and when Lars made his way down the tunnel after the 3–0 defeat, about seven or eight feet away from me, I could see no pain, no fury in his face, just sadness.

After the goal that took the score to 2–0 I was completely finished. Please let it all be over soon, I prayed – and I still had 78 minutes to go. I'd never made such a terrible mistake in the six years since I started as a goalkeeper again in Neitersen. And I had to make a blunder like that in the only game of mine ever to have been shown on German

television. I'd even called my mother to tell her, 'I'm going to be on ARD on Sunday.' It meant a lot to me for someone in Germany to know what I'd achieved in England. At half-time I said to myself, 'OK, now pull yourself together.' But it didn't work. I heard the Tottenham fans shouting, 'Dodgy keeper, dodgy keeper!' And I could have shouted along with them.

Thorsten Winkler was waiting, as agreed, by the tunnel to do his interview with Lars. The first question was asked not by the television journalist but by the goalkeeper.

'Could you do me a favour? You can show that stupid second goal in slow motion hundreds of times, I can see that you've got to do that, but could you please leave out all those terrible goal-kicks?'

'Of course we will,' said Winkler.

But the negative impression created by the second goal was so powerful that when he got back to ARD Winkler was asked whether it had really been worth sending a camera crew to England to film a goalkeeper like that.

For Danny Wilson, the humiliation didn't come to an end with the final whistle. When he showed up at the press conference at White Hart Lane the journalists barely paid him any attention. Was it because they were only interested in the team that had won? Or was it their way of showing Wilson how insulted they felt? They had built him and his team up for a week only to see the whole thing collapse like a house of cards.

Happy are those sportsmen who can forget, or at least repress, the memory of bad days. After painful defeats they all say, 'We've got to look forward, not back.' But there aren't many who can really do that. Lars Leese thought he was getting better at it. He was still irritated when other players, even the manager, tried to pin the blame on individuals in the dressing-room after the game, but after six months in Barnsley in the course of which he had been personally blamed two or three times for goals he couldn't have done much about, he understood the system. Blaming others was an attempt to protect oneself against self-doubt. 'The whole team played disastrously badly,' he said when we spoke on the phone after the Tottenham game. 'After all, we barely got over the halfway line. And we left them all that space at the back.' It was all true – although of course it wasn't the whole truth about the defeat.

Daniela and the newborn baby were already out of hospital, Christmas was just around the corner, and that helped Lars to distract himself. On 26 December in Bolton, he'd do better.

In that kind of situation, training can be a kind of escape. Lars immersed himself in his work, throwing himself at shots in the hope that he might rid himself of his anger and doubt. On the afternoon of Tuesday 23 December, he and Watson had another special training session with the goalkeeping coach, and Lars was so ravenous when he got home that he devoured a whole roast chicken all by himself. Two hours later his guts were in a state of rebellion. His body couldn't hold anything down, and he developed a fever. Food poisoning.

It wasn't until Friday, a day before the game in Bolton, that he made it back to the training ground. He told Danny Wilson, 'I can't do it.'

'Are you sure?'

'I can hardly stand up. How am I going to play football?'

He went along to Bolton, but only to watch from the

stand. Being a spectator hurt almost as much as his stomach did. It would have been a good match in which to rehabilitate himself: it ended in a 1–1 draw and Watson hadn't had a lot to do. Once, when Bolton's Icelandic defender Gudni Bergsson got the ball 40 yards out from Barnsley's goal, Lars yelled 'Shoot, shoot!' He was just having a laugh with his colleagues in the stands, but then Bergsson really did shoot, from 40 yards, straight into the net. Lars shut up, though he was sure he'd have saved it.

He had to sit out the 1–0 victory over Derby County on 28 December as well. When they played Bolton again on 3 January 1998, this time in the third round of the FA Cup, Lars turned up fit for duty. Wilson put him back in the stand again.

'Is he round the bend?' asked Markstedt. 'Why isn't he putting a keeper on the subs' bench? What if something happens to Watson?'

Lars had no answer for him. The manager hadn't explained his decision, and Lars didn't have the courage to ask.

It could only have been something personal. The manager had already seen David Watson getting injured at the beginning of the season, and me having to go in goal – how could he risk going into the match without a substitute goalkeeper? My only explanation is that he thought I had been pretending to have food poisoning as a way of going into hiding after that terrible game against Tottenham. And now he wanted to pay me back. When I called in sick, he looked at me and just asked, 'Are you sure?' I thought, 'He doesn't believe me.' A big guy like that doesn't get knocked out by a chicken. But I swear, I really was ill. I could barely move. I'm not a malingerer.

Seven days later, with an away game against West Ham around the corner, Wilson still wouldn't put Lars on the bench. 'No,' Danny Wilson said four years later in his manager's office at Second Division Bristol City's ground, 'I never doubted for a second that Lars was sick. I'd only been working with him for six months, but my image of him was quite clear: he wasn't the kind to run away when things weren't going well.'

But what manager would go into a match voluntarily without a substitute goalkeeper?

'I took a gamble,' he said. 'In the Premier League you can nominate five substitute players. Because I was doing without a substitute goalkeeper, I had more options for midfield or attack. Of course it was a risk, but that was the only reason.'

At the end of February, Wilson did play another two games without a substitute goalkeeper, against Coventry and in the Cup against Manchester United. And at that point in time no one could have imagined he wanted to pay Lars back for anything. So it seems quite plausible that it was nothing more than a tactical gamble.

'Lars could have come to me and I'd have explained it to him,' said Wilson. He was kitted out in the favourite leisurewear of all football managers: T-shirt, shorts, tennis socks and flipflops. 'But players don't like going to the manager to be told why they aren't in the team. They're scared of hearing something negative, and they'd rather cobble together an explanation of their own. Footballers are very insecure creatures. I know that very well. I used to be one myself.'

By mid-January Lars was back on the subs' bench. But was that a reason to be pleased? A month earlier he had been Barnsley's number one – and things were going to stay like that for the rest of the season, even manager Danny Wilson thought so. Now everything had changed again. Watson had secured his place with good performances against Derby and in the Cup against Bolton, and the manager had finally had enough of switching the two around. A rotten chicken had indeed thrown Lars out of the line-up.

Daniela got it into her head that it was her fault. 'I made crazy accusations against myself. I was the one who had got him the chicken from the supermarket.' She ended up convincing herself that she should have tasted the chicken beforehand. Then she would have been sick by the time Lars came home and 'he'd never even have touched the chicken, and would still be number one in Barnsley'. Her husband didn't take the setback quite as badly. Lars had played 11 matches so far. Looked at soberly, that was more than he could have hoped for when he arrived in June. After all, six months ago he had only been playing reserve-team football. But that mood never lasted long. Moments later he'd be thinking, 'But a month ago you played at Anfield.' Still, Lars was always good at looking on the bright side and he quickly turned himself into Watson's loyal adjutant. Some day, somehow, he would get his chance again.

But he could no longer rely on Watson's weakness. That quickly became apparent in January and February 1998. The nervous and over-motivated Watson, who raced out for balls he could never get to, existed only in the videos from the start of the season; the David Watson of early 1998 was one of the best goalkeepers in the Premier League. To a considerable degree, Barnsley owed their victories in the FA Cup – against Tottenham and Manchester United – to Watson's acrobatics. 'It may not be much use to Lars,' said Wilson, 'but from my point of view his commitment paid off fully in the spring when he stopped playing. It was his daily training with Lars, their perpetual competition, that made David an excellent goalkeeper.'

By mid-March, everything seemed possible in Barnsley. Even staying in the Premier League. It could no longer be ignored: Barnsley could play football. Skipper Neil Redfearn dominated midfield and his free-kicks found the back of the net, one after another. Striker Ashley Ward was a thorn in the side of opposing defenders. In Scott Jones, and above all in Chris Morgan whose enormous physique made him look like something out of Dr Frankenstein's laboratory, Danny Wilson had found two young players who were as keen and hungry as they were talented and obsessed. From mid-January to mid-March the squad lost only three out of 12 games. After a 4–3 victory over Southampton on 14 March, Barnsley were in 18th place – still in the relegation zone but equal on points with Tottenham, the club immediately above them. As soon as the final whistle went, club chairman John Dennis dashed into the dressing-room and announced that he was paying for the team to go to Majorca for a week. They'd be setting off the following morning.

'In the middle of the season?' Lars asked Jan Aage Fjörtoft.

'Some clubs do that in England,' explained the Norwegian, a veteran of Swindon Town, Middlesbrough and Sheffield United. 'It's to recharge your batteries – compensation for the lack of a winter break here.'

A little sun certainly wouldn't do any harm, Lars reckoned. They could get down to some decent training in the warmth of Majorca.

'OK,' said Danny Wilson when they arrived at their hotel in Palma de Mallorca. 'Have a nice week. I'll see you on the flight back on Friday.'

Lars felt like a fool. Was he the only one who hadn't

understood what kind of a trip this was going to be? He'd brought his training kit with him, but no clothes to go out in.

'Are we not training at all?' he asked Fjörtoft.

Fjörtoft laughed. 'You could always go jogging on your own.'

A few of the footballers played golf during the day. Lars spent his time in the hotel pool with most of the others. The first beer was ordered in the afternoon.

'Mike, we've got to do something about my thigh,' said Ashley Ward to physiotherapist Michael Tarmey as they sat by the pool. Ward had torn a muscle fibre while sprinting against Southampton. They talked about treatments.

In the evening, taxis were ordered and the whole team went to Magaluf. Tens of thousands of Brits went to this beach resort every summer, most of them with three goals in mind: sex, booze and sunshine. In mid-March, however, the hotels were empty. There was music on in the bars and nightclubs, but hardly anyone there to listen to it. But the footballers of Barnsley FC were determined to ignore the desperate atmosphere. Evening after evening they stood in lifeless pubs and acted as though the places were throbbing with life. They ordered one round of beer after another. Clinton Marcelle, the little king of Barnsley, paid for them all. He had collected 5,000 pesetas from each player before-hand. That made paying simpler, he had told his colleagues. Of course he didn't tell the barman, or the two or three lonely women whose drinks he paid for, where all the banknotes in his wallet came from.

After the fifth or sixth drink the mood actually lightened. Defender Matty Appleby and winger Martin Bullock started fighting.

★   ★   ★

Ashley Ward was missing from the next game, against Liverpool. Barnsley's most important striker had not recovered from his torn muscle. But Barnsley showed no signs of suffering either from his absence or from the hardships of the Majorca trip. They played with confidence and determination and took an early lead, courtesy of a Redfearn goal. Even when Liverpool went 2–1 up, thanks to two goals from Karlheinz Riedle, the fans at Oakwell still believed that Barnsley could win.

Then referee Gary Willard stepped in.

'We're always talking about players who can't deal with the pressure of big matches,' said Danny Wilson, 'so why should referees be any different? In the Liverpool game the referee had totally lost it.' During a running duel with Michael Owen, Barnsley's Darren Barnard mistimed a tackle, kicking Liverpool's golden boy in the calf. Willard showed Barnard the red card. Chris Morgan then tried to stop Owen, who that season was revealing his precocious skills for the first time. He tried to grab his shoulder, but Owen was too quick for him and Morgan accidentally caught his face instead. Willard produced another red.

Oakwell was in a fury. The stadium was spewing out bitterness the way a volcano spews lava. The atmosphere started to get to the players. Tackles were aimed at shins rather than the ball. Jan Aage Fjörtoft used a judo hold against a fan who had run on to the pitch in an attempt to reach the referee. It was the best tackle in the match: Fjörtoft took a run, grabbed the man from behind by the throat and pulled him back with such force that his black T-shirt flew up, revealing an enormous white belly. The Norwegian striker ably threw the fan to the floor and lay triumphantly on top of him until the stewards came.

With nine players Barnsley actually managed to pull the

score back to 2–2 after 85 minutes. Had Oakwell ever heard so much noise? 'We are Premier League, say we are Premier League!' Fans ran on to the pitch, and no one could tell whether they wanted to express their joy or their fury. Stewards stopped them and 17 were arrested. Referee Willard ordered the teams to the dressing-rooms. No one knew whether the match had been stopped or merely interrupted.

The teams came back five minutes later, and Steve McManaman scored the winning goal in injury time. Barnsley's Darren Sheridan and Liverpool skipper Paul Ince then exchanged blows. Willard ordered Sheridan off the pitch, Ince went unpunished. None of Barnsley's players or supervisors protested. They were too disheartened.

'It was the day Barnsley lost its innocence – and with its innocence, all its optimism,' said Ian McMillan. As he made his way home from the stadium, he saw people standing around in little groups in the streets, discussing the game. 'Like after a train crash,' McMillan said. 'I walked on and thought, "No, if the Premier League's like that, so anarchic, so unfair, so treacherous, then we don't want it." I'm an easy-going bloke, but that day I completely lost it. That referee ruined our whole season.'

The Liverpool game was Barnsley's turning point. In retrospect, Lars, Wilson and McMillan all agree on that. 'After such an ugly match, who could go on believing that our season was a lovely fairy-tale, with a happy ending around the corner?' asked McMillan. 'After Liverpool it seemed unavoidable: we would be relegated.'

Seven days and two more defeats later, Danny Wilson felt the same way. 'Six games before the end of the season it occurred to me: we're not going to make it,' he said. 'My task was to ensure that the players didn't get a sense of that.'

Fine, he told the team, we're in trouble, but we've just got to win the next game.

They lost 2–1 to Newcastle United.

We've just got to win the next game.

They drew 1–1 with Tottenham Hotspur.

We've just got to win the next game.

They lost 2–0 to Arsenal, and then 1–0 to Leicester City. They were relegated.

Neil Redfearn had the ball when Dermot Gallagher, the referee, blew the final whistle at Filbert Street. Redfearn kicked the ball away and fell to his knees. Striker Andy Liddell threw himself to the ground. Lars had stopped concentrating on the game a quarter of an hour earlier. He'd just sat on the subs' bench feeling that nothing would save them now. The fear of relegation destroyed Barnsley's game. Redfearn, their best player, was constantly losing the ball. That spoke volumes. Instead of following the action on the pitch, Lars watched Barnsley's supporters. They were singing, 'We love you Barnsley, we do!' Even the final whistle, the official confirmation of relegation, didn't stop them.

If they'd cursed us and spat at us, relegation would have been easier to bear. Hearing the fans singing defiantly, as though they were delirious, brought tears to my eyes. I realised how much it would have meant to these people, to the club, to me, if we'd stayed in the Premier League. Realistically speaking, we deserved to be relegated. It took us far too long to get going. For the whole of the first third of the season we hadn't a clue what was going to happen to us. But you still think to yourself – if only we'd held on to that 1–0 lead against Leeds; if only the referee hadn't lost his head against Liverpool . . . could

have, should have . . . By the time we got to the dressing-room at Leicester there was no point speculating. I felt empty, as if someone had torn my brain out. And from outside, through the walls of the stadium, I could still hear them shouting, 'We love you Barnsley, we do!' It was all I could do not to cry.

The game against Manchester United on the last day of the season had long been thought of as a fairy-tale ending. United would need a victory to be champions, Barnsley would need a victory to avoid relegation, and Barnsley would win. That was how thousands of people in Barnsley had imagined things for a whole year.

Now it was nothing but a wake. Barnsley had fluffed their last mathematical chance of staying up on the second-last day of the season at Leicester, and at the same time United had lost their battle for the championship against Arsenal.

Barnsley had reached the end of their year. The almost girlish enthusiasm of the previous summer seemed to be light years away. All the people in the town who had in one way or another participated in Barnsley's year in the spotlight felt as though they had aged a hundred years. They were more mature, more clear-eyed, but also more disillusioned. They were tired.

Barnsley lost their last game in the Premier League 2–0. But the fans celebrated once again. The club mascot, Toby Tyke, in his customary costume of a seven-foot cloth bulldog, did a striptease after the final whistle. Hundreds of spectators stormed the pitch and carried striker Ashley Ward away on their shoulders. Ward was holding up a placard. WE'LL BE BACK it read.

10

A QUARTER OF A MILLION A YEAR!

WHEN BARNSLEY'S SUBSTITUTE striker John Hendric got back from his holiday in Majorca with his wife and four children on the evening of Saturday, 4 July 1998, he heard the phone ringing as he was opening the door. He didn't answer it. He was too busy carrying his suitcases into the house.

The phone went on ringing.

Finally, Hendrie gave in and picked up the receiver. On the line was John Dennis, the Barnsley chairman. He wouldn't keep him for long, Dennis said, he just wanted to ask him if he would be prepared to take on the job of manager at Barnsley.

Luckily, Hendrie had already put the cases down, otherwise he would probably have dropped them. People coming home from holiday are prepared for certain things – a burgled house, a running tap, an overdue credit card bill – but being welcomed by the question of whether or not he fancied becoming his team's manager in two days' time, although he had no coaching experience whatsoever, came as a complete surprise to Hendrie. He would have to sleep on it, he said. Meaning: lie awake brooding.

Five days earlier John Dennis had put a *Barnsley Star* reporter right with vehemence in his voice: 'When will you finally understand that Danny Wilson isn't going anywhere?' And presumably the chairman had believed that Wilson would stay on as Barnsley's manager. Rumours that Sheffield Wednesday wanted to lure away Wilson had been doing the rounds for months. In fact – and Dennis knew this – Wednesday wanted to give the job to Gérard Houllier, the technical director of the French Football Association. But at the end of June the news reached Sheffield that Houllier had signed for Liverpool. Now they were really interested in Wilson. Barnsley's manager had had his best years as a player in Sheffield Wednesday's midfield and the club meant more to him than most; above all, Wednesday gave him the chance to stay in the Premiership. On 1 July, five days before the start of training, Wilson rang Dennis and told him first that, generally speaking, 'football is a jungle. You don't know what's waiting around the next corner,' and in particular that he was moving to the club around the corner – Sheffield Wednesday, 30 miles down the road. That made the chairman's position plain and simple: he had four days to find a new manager. As far as the fans were concerned there was 'only one Danny Wilson', as they were always singing, so it seemed an impossible task to find a satisfactory successor.

'What should I do?' Dennis asked Keith Lodge, the journalist on the *Barnsley Chronicle*. Over the years, Dennis had come to enjoy talking to Lodge. As an outsider, Lodge wasn't scared of being critical, but he always had the club's best interests at heart. Dennis explained to Lodge that the club didn't just need a good manager; more than anything else it needed a manager who would ease the fans' fury over

Wilson's departure. After their promotion to the Premier League Wilson had acquired the status of a miracle-worker, and the team's prompt relegation wouldn't change that. After the final Premier League game Wilson had declared over the Oakwell PA: 'This is Danny Wilson. I just wanted to say I'm going to stay in Barnsley and try to bring the club back into the Premier League.' But that wasn't much help right now. The fans would feel betrayed.

That's why Dennis turned his attention to John Hendrie, better known in Barnsley as Super John, since it was his goals in the 1996/97 campaign that had helped the team go up. The fact that the striker had spent most of the Premier League season sitting on the subs' bench did nothing to diminish that – quite the contrary: at the age of 34 Hendrie was no longer the most valuable player, but he was still very popular with the public. So he was an ideal candidate to keep the fans happy. However, a manager has another task as well, one which is more important: he has to manage the team. And that was a problem, as it would transpire the very next day.

After almost two months off during the summer, most professionals are pleased to get back to work. Barnsley saw promotion back into the Premiership as a realistic goal. The team was practically unchanged, and so were the jokes in the dressing-room when they returned to Oakwell on 6 July for the first day of pre-season training. No one was surprised that Hendrie still wasn't there 15 minutes before the start. He was often late. It only occurred to the players that something was wrong when Peter Shirtliff, the reserve-team coach, came into the dressing-room shortly afterwards and told them they all had to come over to the laundry, which doubled as a conference room. Normally they would discuss tactics there a day before a game, but what kind of tactics were there to sort out ten minutes before the team's first training session?

When John Dennis came in with John Hendrie, Lars immediately understood what was up, but the news was still a surprise for the players. Hendrie would be assuming the managership and at the same time he would be staying on as one of them, Dennis announced.

A player-manager role is unthinkable in Italian or Spanish professional football, because the problems are all too clear. What if the other strikers start complaining when the manager fields himself? How many tactical details are going to escape the manager's notice if he's out there on the pitch? But in England the player-manager was all the rage for a short time at the end of the nineties, after Ruud Gullit led Chelsea to victory in the FA Cup in 1997.

Still, Barnsley's players listened with growing disbelief as Dennis passed on the leadership to Hendrie. He talked about discipline, order and hardness. Lars found himself thinking about a player who had represented all the opposite values the previous year: John Hendrie. Hendrie had played the role of the class clown to the point of self-parody. The first image that always came into my mind when his name was mentioned was of a bright red face without eyebrows. That, he wrote in his autobiography *Don't Call Me Happy*, was how he had once come back from a mini-break with Middlesbrough, for whom he had played for many years. One night when he was lying drunk in bed, his team-mates had shaved off his eyebrows. The next day Hendrie topped off the effect by turning himself lobster-pink in the blazing sun.

And all of a sudden the clown was to be in charge of the circus.

'It'll never work,' Fjørtoft said in passing to Rimmo, the kitman, when the players came back from Hendrie's first meeting.

That was a shock: Hendrie the manager. As he stood in front of us that first time, you could feel an inner resistance stirring in all the players. Many of them sat there with their arms over their chests, or their lips scornfully pressed together. The previous year he hadn't said a single serious word, and all of a sudden he was going on about discipline and order. No one sniggered, but as a player he had never stood out as a great tactician or leader. There are professional footballers, like Matthias Sammer of Borussia Dortmund, who think like managers while they're still players, and actually tell the team what to do, but Hendrie had been the opposite. Who would believe him when he started coming out with clever stuff like 'shift your defence' or 'we're only going to play with one striker this week'? He had no natural authority. I knew things wouldn't get any easier where I was concerned. After his performance over the past six months David Watson was number one anyway, but I had a sense that under Hendrie I would only get a chance if David was injured. Somehow I felt I wasn't really Hendrie's type of goalkeeper. He wasn't keen on me.

The overseas professionals who had felt excluded by the British players on the team were particularly enraged by Hendrie's appointment. They saw him as their greatest tormentor. As a player Hendrie had always been making jokes at their expense. In fact he made fun of everyone and everything, but the foreigners, who were unfamiliar with the piss-taking that went on in English dressing-rooms and who didn't understand a lot of the banter because of their problems with the language, were insecure enough to interpret the jokes as personal attacks. They were worried that as a manager Hendrie would boycott them. And so, as they talked to one another about it, their anxiety mounted. But the English professionals were equally sceptical. Last season Hendrie had still been mucking around with them; now he was going to lead them out of the wilderness? 'The players were wondering, "Who does he think he is?",' said Keith Lodge. 'Overnight, he'd completely cut himself off from them. As far as we journalists were concerned, he was still the nice, funny guy. Super John. But in the team he was going around with this "I'm the boss" attitude. That meant that he achieved the opposite of what he wanted. He wanted recognition and he earned rejection.' Barnsley FC still joked around when they were training, but more out of routine than pleasure.

John Dennis didn't notice the team's pessimism. Or else he refused to notice it. The chairman had other concerns. How would the public react? By Tuesday no one had burned down the stadium. That was something. There was just one sheet hung from the stadium railings: HENDRIE IS JESUS, WILSON IS JUDAS, it said. As a PR stunt, Hendrie's appointment clearly did have the desired effect; his popularity did to some extent make up for the shock of Wilson's resignation. The popular fury was vented on the club receptionists and the *Barnsley Chronicle*. 'Barnsley's supporters were cheated,' Brian Cooper from Hensworth told the *Chronicle*. 'They waited till we'd bought our season tickets and then they let Wilson go!' Steve Lodge, the Premier League referee from Barnsley, abandoned his impartiality to bring a bit of balance to the discussion: 'I don't hold it against the guy [Wilson] for moving on. Anyone with any ambition would have done the same thing.' And editor Keith Lodge appealed in the *Chronicle*: 'Barnsley will have to keep the smile that Danny Wilson put on our faces.' Easier said than done.

★   ★   ★

It took five games before the self-styled favourite for promotion finally enjoyed a victory in the First Division – a rather unconvincing 1–0 result against Oxford United. The fans' enthusiasm trickled away slowly but surely: at the start of the season against West Bromwich Albion Oakwell had been filled nearly to capacity, but only 16,300 fans came to the second home game against Stockport County, and by the time Norwich City arrived for the sixth game of the season, the gate was down to 15,700. Barnsley lost 3–1, and lost the affection of the fans. Right from the start a minority hurled abuse at the players. The full-backs had the worst time of it. They get it in the ear first for logistical reasons – they're the ones nearest to the spectators. By the end the silent majority had joined in with the rest. The final whistle was drowned in furious booing.

In every football stadium there are fans who really come to complain rather than to celebrate, and who feel better if they've been shouting at a player, from a safe distance, telling him he's a useless time-wasting big girl's blouse. For a year, throughout the whole of the Premier League season, the booing brigade hadn't been much in evidence at Oakwell. Now they came into their own again.

'We're back in the real world,' said Hendrie. He was sulking. He wasn't going to do a thing to boost his players' morale, he told journalists. 'They're grown up. They're old enough to stand on their own two feet.' Anyone with ears would have heard a growing gulf between the manager and the team.

Hendrie was at least inventive in his role as player-manager. After wasting a clear chance on goal in a reserve game, he 'looked in the mirror in the dressing-room and gave myself a right bollocking!'

On the Monday after the defeat at the hands of Norwich, goalkeeper Watson didn't come to training. Immediately after the match he had discovered that his right knee was swollen, and he remembered a shooting pain when he'd blocked a ball with his foot. But he'd had to play to the end of the match. Watson thought he'd pulled a tendon, but in fact his meniscus was torn, the doctor in Barnsley General Hospital told him two days later. They'd have to operate. It would be weeks before Watson could play again. Lars Leese was back in goal.

Or was he?

'In goal . . . we'll see tomorrow,' said Hendrie on the Friday when he was going through the line-up a day before the away game against Grimsby Town. Lars thought he was joking. The third-choice keeper, Anthony Bullock, who had transferred to Barnsley from the amateur club Leek Town a year and a half earlier, had enjoyed his status to excess in the town's bars and nightclubs, but he had not yet played a single professional match. Until that moment it had never occurred to Lars that Bullock might be a serious competitor.

Grimsby was barely more than an hour away from Barnsley. Lars had been there once when he wanted to show friends from Germany a nice English fishing village on the North Sea coast. On the map, Grimsby, at the end of the River Humber, had looked like a suitable place, but perhaps he should have taken a look in a guide-book. What he had imagined to be a nice fishing village turned out to be a big industrial town. The only suggestion of fish was the penetrating smell from the cod processing plants.

On the way there in the team bus Lars tried to convince himself that he was going to play. He tried to read the copy of *FHM* that he'd brought along, but his thoughts drifted away. Was Hendrie seriously thinking about putting Bullock in goal? Why did the manager have so little confidence in him? Or did he just not like him? Normally Lars would only tell himself to keep his mind on things during a game, but now he did it on the bus. Concentrate, he thought, concentrate.

They arrived in Grimsby an hour and a half before the start of play. They put their bags in the dressing-room and went to look at the pitch – the usual pre-match routine. Lars and Bullock walked around on the grass on the tips of their black shoes, trying to find bumps or holes, as though they both knew they were going to play. It was only when they were changing that Hendric told Lars in passing, 'You're playing.'

Barnsley won 2–1. Lars was kept pretty busy, but he never really found himself in difficulties. Over the following week the club beat Reading, third last in the table, 3–0 and gained a 4–0 victory over Crystal Palace, who had been relegated along with them from the Premier League four months earlier. The *Barnsley Chronicle* described Lars as 'a candidate for man of the match'.

In situations like that, professional footballers are no different from football supporters: they just need to see a patch of blue in the sky and they think everything's going to be fine. 'It's a long, long season, we may be able to come up the field from behind,' Lars remarked to Keith Lodge. 'We may get a series of good results and then all of a sudden we'll be up in the top group. We have a good chance.' After this interview, three victories in a row were followed by a 1–1 draw in Bristol and a 2–1 defeat at the hands of Bradford. Barnsley were 13th in the table.

After the final whistle in Bradford, Lars had to undergo a drugs test. During the nineties, mistrust had been so rife in sports such as athletics and cycling that anyone who triumphed in anything at all immediately attracted suspicion by dint of winning alone. But there had never been a serious drugs debate in football. Allegations that Serie A clubs had been deliberately doping their players had been pursued only half-heartedly by the law, the sports associations and the media. Football was the great popular spectacle; if bad things happened, no one wanted to know. To put their consciences at ease, the football organisations tested two players per team at each professional match, but footballers who were caught could generally expect to be punished fairly leniently. In 2000, the Nuremberg midfielder Thomas Ziemer received a six-month ban for testing positive for nandralone. An athlete would have got one or two years for the same thing.

Where drugs were concerned, Barnsley had the dubious pleasure of having been the first high-profile case. In November 1997, amphetamines were found in the urine of Dean Jones, a 20-year-old defender from their reserve team, and Jones was banned for three months. The fact that he'd taken the drug not for a match but for a long night out in a club may say something about Barnsley's night-life, but didn't count as a mitigating circumstance. Jones's amphetamines are believed to have come from an Ecstasy tablet. When I met him with Lars in a bar in Barnsley a few months later, he had clearly learned his lesson: this time Jones stuck to beer.

Lars stood in the test area at Bradford and couldn't produce a thing. The two checkers stared at his penis to see how he was doing – not a drop. He knocked back quantities of beer and apple juice and waited for his body to spring into action.

Suddenly I started to panic. It occurred to me to my horror that I'd smoked a fat joint during the summer holidays. I'd been on holiday with Danny in the Caribbean, and when we were taking a water taxi to a small island the driver asked us if we wanted to buy some grass. 'Come on,' I said to Danny, 'Caribbean, beach – if not here, where? Let's try it.'

It was only once I was back in Bradford that I remembered that marijuana was on the list of forbidden drugs, and that French International goalkeeper Fabien Barthez had been banned because of it. My hands were completely sweaty. I had no idea how long marijuana persists in the urine.

Twenty minutes later, he finally managed a sample. As he left, one of the checkers told him amicably that he would be sent the result in three weeks' time.

Three weeks is long enough to convince yourself that you're going to be suspended for testing positive. In English football, even cigarette smoking is seen as a big taboo. At Leverkusen there were five or six smokers on the team, and although Christoph Daum mightn't have approved, he openly tolerated it. The smoking seats were at the front of the team bus, and the non-smoking section was from the middle to the back. When Lars had lit a Marlboro Light during his first evening with Barnsley in the beer garden, his team-mate Darren Sheridan asked him furiously, 'What, you smoke, do you?'

'Take a look at yourself,' replied Lars.

Sheridan, who was halfway through his sixth pint, hadn't the faintest idea what Lars was talking about. Beer is duty. Cigarettes are poison. A rule of football in Barnsley.

On team trips, Lars and South African player Eric Tinkler only ever smoked secretly in their rooms. They hung the complimentary hotel shower-caps over the smoke alarms in the ceiling.

After three weeks, Sean McClare, the second Barnsley player to have been tested in Bradford, got his letter. Result: negative. Lars' letter didn't arrive.

It showed up the next day. Some companies are said to

do that after job interviews: sending out the acceptances one day, rejections the next. In the case of Lars Leese it was a whim on the part of the Post Office that made him quake for a day. His test result was negative too.

However much the club tried to turn the smallest triumphs into heralds of the great turnaround, the next setback was sure to be on its way. After their 2–0 defeat on 11 October to relegation candidates Port Vale, both manager and players were irritable, not to say aggressive. The encounter had been broadcast live on Sky Sport, giving the whole of England an opportunity to check out Barnsley's plummeting performance. The following Monday at training in the gym, Hendrie yelled at defender Matty Appleby in front of all the other players, asking him what he had been thinking about when the first goal had been scored. Appleby had tried to head the ball back to Lars, 12 yards behind him, but the ball had slipped over his head; Port Vale's Martin Foyle was a grateful recipient of his weak glanced header. Appleby shouted back at Hendrie that Lars should have told him Foyle was lurking behind him. Lars couldn't defend himself, he was out on the pitch having goalkeeping coaching. Later, on the way home, Peter Markstedt told him what had happened.

'There was a terrible atmosphere,' said Markstedt. 'Everyone was talking behind everyone else's back, everyone needed someone to shift the blame on to. On the training ground the players were yelling at one another. The idea of self-criticism was completely beyond them.'

The next morning, John Hendrie called Lars into his office. He showed him the first goal on video.

'I can't hear you shouting,' said Hendrie.

'There were 16,000 spectators in the stadium, no one would've heard me shouting.'

'You're the size of a tree, I could hear you shouting at the coast,' retorted Hendrie, who could himself, by now, have been heard some considerable distance away.

'What does it matter whether I shout or whether I don't, it doesn't alter the fact that Matty's header was far too weak. No keeper in the world could have prevented that goal.'

'But if you fucking well shout, he won't even fucking try to head the fucking ball back to you.'

'But heading it back was the right thing to do. The header just wasn't good enough.'

'You've got to fucking shout! A bloke the size of a tree and I can't hear you! Look, I'm going to play you the fucking video again and you'll see!'

'You know, John, I've had enough of this. If it helps you to mark someone out as a scapegoat, then I'll take responsibility for the goal. Although no normal person would ever have dreamed of blaming the goalkeeper.'

Lars left the office without waiting for an answer or saying goodbye.

He was sure that Hendrie wouldn't put him in the line-up the following Saturday.

It's something I would never do today: shoulder the blame. You just weaken your own position. The next disputed goal you let in, someone's going to try to finger you again. At some point everyone's going to keep getting at you, whether it's justified or not, and you're the scapegoat who's out of the team. I'm always in favour of people being honest and straight-forward with each other, but unfortunately that isn't necessarily how things are in a football team. So it doesn't do you any harm to develop a protective skin

**of arrogance, so that all the accusations bounce off
it. I learned that – for my next life.**

Lars did play the following Saturday. Objectively speaking, that had always been on the cards, but like most foreign
players Lars always feared the worst from Hendrie. The goalkeeper was convinced that the manager was just waiting for
the opportunity to get rid of him. In fact, Hendrie wasn't
malicious; he was just an inexperienced manager who was
floundering in the face of failure. Striker Jan Aage Fjörtoft
didn't really listen to him during his half-time pep-talks now,
concentrating instead on how many times he said the word
'fuckin''. Thirty-two times in five minutes, Fjörtoft claimed.

Lars had one of his better games against Sheffield United,
but cut an unhappy figure when a free-kick flew past him as
he slipped in the appalling rain and fell headlong into the
mud. Despite the irritating equaliser, the 1–1 draw filled everyone with optimism. Three days later, all the hope had gone.
Barnsley said goodbye to the 1998/99 season with a 3–0 loss
to Tranmere Rovers on a cold, wet October evening. They
still had more than half the season to go, but in Tranmere the
dream that this team and this manager might achieve something together was revealed as an illusion. Barnsley had none
of the things you need for a successful football team: commitment, sound tactics, energy, courage, not to mention elegance
and vision. It was their worst match for two years. 'I sat in the
grandstand and thought, "Hendrie's lost the support of his
players. They've stopped playing for him,"' said Keith Lodge.

By half-time, the team sitting in the dressing-room had
lost the will to play. John Hendrie was in despair. He knew
that their performance amounted to a vote of no confidence
in him. 'It was a slap in the face for me,' he said later. His
desperation turned into panic, his panic into fury. Hendrie

lost his head. His face turned scarlet, his lips were white, his nostrils flared. He ranted and raged and lost all self-control. He picked up a plastic litre-bottle of Lucozade and threw it against the wall with all his might. A few inches to the left and it would have hit Jan Aage Fjörtoft's head.

At home in Barnsley, Daniela got a phone call. An unfamiliar voice at the other end said he was going to kill her husband, then put the phone down. Lars had the second goal on his conscience. It was a difficult shot, but it went in the near corner. Goalkeepers are supposed to be able to save shots to the near corner. That's a rule of thumb. After the game a furious John Dennis marched over to the dressing-rooms. He ordered Hendrie into the corridor and gave him a sound bollocking.

Outwardly, Barnsley seemed undaunted and went on turning itself into a model club. With the money the club had earned in the Premiership, a new training centre was built right next to the stadium. The uninviting area where visiting supporters had had to stand in the rain became a steeply raked, roofed grandstand, and the generous dressing-rooms were equipped with the latest facilities such as a fitness studio and a massage room. But out on the pitch, Barnsley, the 'people's club', the nation's favourite outsider, had turned within three months into a very ordinary First Division team; and sometimes, as in Tranmere, they couldn't even manage to be ordinary.

After Tranmere, Barnsley should really have fired John Hendrie, but that wasn't John Dennis's style. He had been connected with the club for more than 40 years, having taken over the chairmanship from his father Ernest. He was convinced that things were best left as they were. Barnsley had a brass band that played at home games, and the manager's office still looked like an elderly aunt's living-room, with a fat, burgundy-coloured carpet and an electric convector heater. In short, it was a club that prided itself on its honesty. John Dennis wanted to have as little as possible to do with all the madness of modern professional football: the hectic sale of players, the ruthless dismissal of managers. Hendrie could stay where he was.

On 24 October, four days after the Tranmere game, the player-manager changed half the line-up for a home game against Portsmouth. He put new players in five positions, took himself out of the team and put Anthony Bullock in goal in place of Lars Leese.

'I was surprised,' said Keith Lodge. 'And so were the fans. Lars was this giant dominating the penalty area, and even if he didn't reckon the second goal of Tranmere was entirely clean, he hadn't played a single bad game. Bullock, on the other hand, had no experience whatsoever in professional football.' David Watson, whose August meniscus crisis had turned into an apparently endless nightmare, was astonished. 'I wasn't there for every game because I was spending a lot of time in hospital and in rehab, but in the matches that I saw Lars didn't really do anything wrong. I figured he deserved to play for the whole season. Certainly Bullock wasn't a better goalkeeper than Lars.' Assistant manager Eric Winstanley, who was born in Barnsley in 1944 and had spent 33 of his 54 years with the club, was recovering at home from a heart attack. The news he was hearing from Oakwell did little to put his mind at rest. 'The club wasn't strong at that point in time. The manager was still trying to find his way, and he changed the team around a hell of a lot, from top to bottom. Players of undisputed quality were thrown into doubt. Lars was one example. I was astonished when I heard that Bullock had replaced him.' The only one who didn't seem surprised by the move was Lars himself. Ever since Hendrie had left him on tenterhooks before his first game of the season in Grimsby, the keeper had been getting used to the idea that his days were numbered under the new manager. Sometimes the thought would go away for a few days, even weeks, but it always came back. At some point Hendrie was going to get rid of him.

Barnsley redeemed themselves for the amateurish display against Tranmere with a hard-fought 2–1 win over Portsmouth. Bullock acquitted himself particularly well; in fact, his first professional game would be the best of his short career. But no one could have known that then. It was clear at the time that after a performance like that Bullock had the right to go on playing.

At the beginning of December, the club's directors stated pretty clearly that they expected nothing more of the present season by authorising the sale of Barnsley's best player, striker Ashley Ward, to Blackburn Rovers for £4.5 million – a record sum for Barnsley. Financial considerations had become more important than sporting ambitions, which, in view of the team's prospects, was completely understandable. There wasn't all that much difference between ending up 10th or 15th in the table.

Almost at the same time as Ward, Jan Aage Fjörtoft transferred to Bundesliga club Eintracht Frankfurt. Fjörtoft had already told Hendrie he wanted to leave the club in September. 'What kind of chance have I got if you're the player-manager?' Fjörtoft had told him. 'You're always going to play yourself rather than me.' By December there was an uneasy truce between the striker and the player-manager, and much else that was uneasy too. For what had begun as an argument about a tackle on the training ground between Fjörtoft and Darren Sheridan had soon turned into a violent scrap in the dressing-room.

Fjörtoft, known to his team-mates as 'fat arse', was not

much liked by most of the other players. Not only was he more intelligent than most' of them, he was also unusually free with his opinions. 'The man who knew all the answers,' kitman Rimmo called him. As a goal-poacher who spent a lot of time doing little, but often turned up in the right place at the right time, he had won himself a decent reputation in five years of playing for English clubs. He would play no better in Frankfurt and he would still be celebrated as a hero.

In England, players are expected to be modest in interviews, to talk about how lucky they were when they scored that fantastic goal and how hard the whole team had been working. In England, more than anywhere else, Fjörtoft irritated his team-mates with his big mouth. In Germany, on the other hand, an average player can become a great star if he can hold his own as an entertainer in the showbiz world of the Bundesliga. After Fjörtoft had, unbelievably, managed to avoid relegation with Frankfurt, he spontaneously planted a great smacker on the lips of the lady mayoress Petra Roth as they stood in the VIP stand. Fjörtoft remarked, 'I hope she's a better mayor than she is a kisser.'

Before leaving Barnsley, Fjörtoft told Lars about his final conversation with Hendrie. 'He told me he didn't mind me going because he wanted the foreigners out of the team anyway.' There is some doubt as to whether or not Hendrie actually said that, but after his own experiences with the manager it seemed entirely believable to Lars. It confirmed the gloomy direction his thoughts were taking.

After I talked to Fjörtoft it was clear to me that I didn't have a chance in Barnsley any more. I went training, I showered, on Saturday I took warm-up kicks at Bullock, watched the game, showered, went home. I didn't care whether we won or lost. I felt

nothing at all. I was completely apathetic. You can be a substitute goalkeeper and still feel that you belong. I'd felt like that at Leverkusen, and during my first year with Barnsley. But by now I no longer felt as though being a professional footballer was really a dream job. I was part of a team in which no one gave a damn, in which players punched one another in the dressing-room out of frustration, in a town that had been red and white when I arrived and where now the people booed us. And to top it all, the manager preferred a goalkeeper who I knew was worse than I was. It was all dragging me down. I felt humiliated.

In January 1999, Hendrie called Lars into his office. His contract ran out at the end of June, the manager said. He just wanted to tell him it wouldn't be renewed.

'OK,' said Lars, 'that's good to know.'

When Daniela learned that she would be moving out of Barnsley in six months' time, she felt differently. A year and a half earlier, when she had first arrived in England, she had wept she was so desperate to leave; now she wanted to stay put. 'I felt that this was my home,' she said. 'Our friends and all the children in our street; the people in Royston, who were so warm and hospitable. I'd realised that when I'd lost my fear of speaking English. I didn't want to give it up.'

Her husband called his agent Tony Woodcock to ask him to keep an eye out for a new club.

'No problem,' said Woodcock.

Lars was realistic enough to know better: it was a big problem. He was a reserve goalkeeper behind a below-average keeper in a mid-table First Division team. What club would want someone like him?

Daniela noticed how much Lars' facial expressions had changed. 'During his first year in Barnsley he had always been happy when he came home, even if he was exhausted from training. In the second year he just looked tired. Lars isn't the kind of man to show his anger. He went on trying to be jolly and nice to everyone. But all it meant was that I felt so alone in my fury with the club and the manager.'

She still went to the occasional game at Oakwell, but whenever she found herself standing in the VIP lounge with Lars' friends Ales Krizan and Peter Markstedt, both of whom had been injured and out of action for some time, she said loudly what a crap club it was, what a cliquey business. She hoped someone from the committee was standing nearby. It wasn't that she believed she would improve Lars' situation by doing so, but at least she hoped to be heard.

One day, Lars began to stick up for himself, even if it was just to pass the time. June was too far away to go on playing the loyal sub. He decided to make life difficult for Bullock. He stopped giving him tips. He stopped being friendly to him. Every time they went for training he made sure Bullock was aware which of them was the better goalkeeper. Lars' saves, his body language, everything was designed to express both total determination and profound contempt for his rival. When kicking warm-ups to Watson before the game, he had tried to direct the balls in such a way that Watson would get to them, to boost his confidence: with Bullock, he tried to send him as many unsaveable shots as possible. When he had sent yet another ball flying into the net, Lars apologised to Bullock. 'Oh, sorry, I forgot you weren't good enough for shots like that.'

There are a number of stories about substitute goalkeepers putting their superiors off their game in this way. Oliver Kahn was up against the gifted Polish player Alexander

Famulla when he began his career at the age of 19 with Bundesliga team Karlsruhe SC. When Famulla 'got it in the neck from the newspapers' during a brief out-of-form phase, Kahn recalled, 'I got a move on. I realised he wasn't up to it, he was fragile.' There were endless rows, said Kahn, and then Famulla was out. There's a story among professional goalkeepers that Dutch keeper Ronald Waterreus used to turn on the television in the middle of the night to make sure that his room-mate and rival at PSV Eindhoven Georg Koch didn't sleep a wink before a game.

Lars used Toni Schumacher's autobiography *Anpfiff* (*Kick-off*) as a kind of manual for the games he played with Bullock. But perhaps that was the problem: he needed instructions. He wasn't ruthless by nature and had to overcome his own personality in order to be a bastard. Could it be that he wasn't convincing in that role? Maybe Bullock just had nerves of steel. At any rate, in line with his talent, he went on to have a decent season. By the end of February, when Bullock had 26 matches under his belt and no changes were in sight, Lars came to terms with his fate.

'When I talk about that time, it sounds as though I'm talking about being in jail,' said Peter Markstedt, who was himself fighting to get back into the first team after a severe back injury. 'The manager just sat in his office looking grumpy. Players like myself and Lars tried to spin out our work quota until our contracts ran out. We were waiting for it all to be over.'

Alex McLeish was the name of the man who came to Lars' rescue. The manager was in the process of leading Hibernian out of the Scottish First Division and into the Premier Division, and Tony Woodcock had been given a wink that McLeish was planning to ditch his unpredictable Icelandic goalkeeper Olafur Gottskalsson when they went up. When Woodcock told McLeish that Lars Leese might be able to help Hibernian, the manager vaguely remembered watching television a year earlier when Sky Sports expert Trevor Francis had tried out his German pronunciation and reported 'a brilliant save from Lars Lasso'.

In March, Lars flew to Edinburgh for a three-day trial, including a game with Hibernian's reserve team against Ayr United. By the time the final whistle blew, Lars was sure he had played one of his best games in Britain. In the course of his team's 3–1 victory he had managed to save a number of long-distance shots and had seen off several threats with some courageous runs off his line. All his goal-kicks were successful too, which was sure to have made an impression. British football was obsessed with goal-kicks; the English could talk endlessly about the speed and accuracy with which a keeper could kick the ball. In the mid-nineties, during his time at Manchester City, the German national goalkeeper Eike Immel wondered 'whether goal-kicks are the only thing managers and experts in England find remotely interesting in a goalkeeper'. At City, they made him practise hundreds of them every time he trained, 'as though I was 14'. He was in fact 35. 'And the only thing it got me is arthritis in the hip.'

The day after the reserve game, Lars trained once again with the first team, and afterwards McLeish called him into his office. He was impressed, the manager said, with the calm and confidence Lars had radiated during the game against Ayr. 'We'll call Tony Woodcock, and then we'll discuss everything else.' It had been a while since football had made Lars so happy. 'See you soon,' Hibernian's manager said by way of goodbye – the usual cliché, but this time Lars believed him.

When he arrived home in Royston, Daniela greeted him with great excitement. Woodcock had rung four times. Hibernian wanted him.

Lars rang back.

'It's fine, Lars. They called me, they're keen.'

'That's fantastic. I'll be there right away.'

'Fine, no problem. I'll sort out the money side of things over the next few days, and then draw up a contract.'

'What do you reckon I can make there?'

'Quarter of a million a year.'

'Tony, we're talking about Scotland here.'

'Yes, but there's no transfer fee involved, so you'll get a bonus. £4,000 a week, three-year contract – it won't be a problem.'

A week later, Tony Woodcock had sorted everything out.

'I've talked to them,' he said to Lars. 'It's not happening. They've lost a sponsor.'

'What? It sounded as though everything was in the bag.'

'It was, but now they haven't got the money. The whole thing's off, I'm afraid. We'll find something else, OK? We'll do that.'

I couldn't believe it. As far as I was concerned the deal was all done and dusted. I'd trained well in Edinburgh, and I'm not just saying that, it's true. The kitman – and you've always got to be in with him – had said, 'Don't worry, we'll be seeing each other again,' and the manager was going to call Woodcock and everything would be sorted within the week. It didn't happen.

Lars couldn't stop thinking about why it hadn't worked out. He gave Hibernian a call, even though footballers don't do that kind of thing. They don't phone another club's manager, even after a failed transfer; they let their agent do the talking, they allow themselves to be chucked from one club to another 'like a piece of meat', as the world-class Dutch defender Jaap Stam said when he was transferred, against his will, in autumn 2001 from Manchester United to Lazio. They make a lot of money, but they ask no questions. Whatever happens to them, they put up with it.

The Hibernian secretary told Lars that Alex McLeish was unavailable. He called five times, and each time the secretary told him the manager was in a meeting; he was on the training ground; he was out of the office. By the sixth call Lars was clearly becoming a nuisance. He was put through.

'I just wanted to know why the transfer didn't happen.'

Unfortunately, McLeish had simply changed his mind. He was perfectly amicable about the whole thing. Things like that just happen in football. He shouldn't take it too badly.

Even today, Lars still can't understand why the transfer collapsed. I called Woodcock to talk about it. I had already interviewed him a number of times in my role as a journalist, and as always he was friendly and polite – more friendly and polite than most people in the football business. When I told him I wanted to talk to him about Lars Leese, he told me to call him in a few days' time as he was in the car. Over the coming weeks I called him six more times. He told me to call back in half an hour; half an hour later he was in a meeting; later he was out on the pitch and told me to call him at the office first thing next morning; next morning I got his voice-mail. I gave up.

It could be that he was just very busy. He had, after all, recently started working as sports director for Eintracht Frankfurt. It could be that he just didn't want to talk about his work with Lars Leese. Lars himself met Woodcock again in the summer of 2001 when they were playing in an Old Boys' charity game in Cologne.

So you just say hello, amicably enough, and chat for a moment or two. No point in collaring him about it two years on, so I leave him in peace.

By mid-April 1999, Lars was no longer sure whether Woodcock was aware of how serious things were. For six weeks, since his trial for Hibs, Lars had heard nothing more concrete from his agent than 'No problem, we'll sort it out' or 'I might have something in Norway.' On the evening of Friday 16 April Barnsley played Sunderland, so the week-end was free. Lars flew to Cologne to make it clear to Woodcock how much he needed his help. He was running out of time. In three weeks' time the English season would be over.

They met on the Saturday in the Geissbockheim, before Cologne played Fortuna in the town derby in the Müngersdorf Stadium. Admittedly it was only Zweite Bundesliga football, but the Cologne football scene was pretty much self-contained, and the fans saw the match as the event of the year. Anyone who was anybody was in the stadium. Lars found Woodcock in the company of former FC Cologne stars, big and small, and the most prominent Cologne sporting agents, Wolfgang Fahrian and Wolfgang Thielen, were there too. Most of them were behaving as though they were all the best of friends, and they were determined to prove it with backslapping, hugs and jovial laughter.

It was in that atmosphere that Lars reminded Woodcock that he simply had to find a club. He had a family to feed, after all. 'I'm on hot coals, Tony. All this uncertainty is killing me. Am I going to sell the house? What am I going to do with my furniture? I'd like to put all this behind me.'

'Fine, we'll sort something out. Wolfgang, I've got a goal-keeper here – have you got anything for him?'

'A goalie?' Fahrian replied. Give me his name and I'll sort something out for him.'

Lars flew back to England feeling that he had done everything he could. He had emphatically asked Woodcock to get to work on it. All he could do now was wait.

When Lars turned up for training on Monday, John Dennis paid the team a visit and called for silence. The club had just fired John Hendrie, the chairman said. 'We'll have to see, perhaps the new manager will extend your contract after all,' Dennis added when he met Lars alone in the office after training. It was just something to say, though, Lars knew it. Nonetheless, he told me about it a few days later, as though all of a sudden there might just possibly be a chance of staying with Barnsley. He was clutching at the most unlikely prospects. That was how desperate he was.

At home, Lars hid his worries about the future well behind his habitual calm; anyway, Daniela was too preoccupied with the idea of having to leave. 'I cycled through Royston or took Vivian to nursery school, and all of a sudden I wanted to cry because I kept thinking, "This is the last time you're going to see this avenue, soon you won't be able to come here any more." It was so painful that I didn't even wonder all that much about where we were going to go. My fear was: we've got to get out of here!'

In May, Lars went on one final trip with Barnsley. Once again he fired warm-up shots at Tony Bullock and watched unemotionally as Barnsley played their last, unimportant game of the season against Swindon. Whatever they did that season, they never seemed to get any higher than 13th place in the table, and that was the way it ended. Lars had been the German giant, the hero of Liverpool. He had played 20 games – eight in the Premier League, eight in the First Division and four in the League Cup – and now he was going, quietly, with no flowers, no mention in the papers and no hug from his team-mates. He simply vanished from Barnsley's life. At the rather cool end-of-season dinner in the Ardsley House Hotel he shook hands with the players who happened to be nearby, or who were his friends. 'Take care,' said assistant manager Eric Winstanley, who was temporarily in charge of the team after Hendrie's dismissal. The other foreigners who had come with him, like Peter Markstedt and Eric Tinkler, stayed on for another year. They had signed three-year contracts in 1997 – an opportunity Lars had turned down. 'We'd better make it two years,' he had said. It's terrible to leave when you'd rather stay.

On their last afternoon in Barnsley, the Leeses held a leaving party for Vivian, Christopher and all the children of the neighbourhood. At the end they played 'Goodbye' by the Spice Girls, and one girl hurled herself tearfully at Daniela, sobbing as she told her not to go. Then the two of them sobbed together.

'The next morning, when we set off with the car packed to the roof and drove down Winter Avenue, everything seemed as though it was in slow motion. The words kept drumming through my head: I don't want to go, I don't want to go,' said Daniela.

At the leaving party, I had also realised more than ever how much at home we were in Barnsley now. And now I had to set off with no notion of where I would be next season. But at that moment I was just happy to be leaving. Happy that something was finally moving, even if it was only our car.

11

NO PROBLEM, NO PROBLEM

IN MID-JUNE 1999, Lars took his family to Holland, hoping, for once, that his holiday would be disturbed – by Tony Woodcock. He tried not to show that his thoughts were elsewhere as he and the children visited a farm and admired the pigs and chickens.

June is the silly season of professional football. Like the players, the managers and coaches go on holiday. Afterwards many of them find themselves wondering what on earth made them think they could find peace during that month of all months. Ideally, professional clubs have made all their staffing decisions for the coming season by April, but that ideal has nothing to do with reality. Because many clubs don't know until mid-May whether they're going to stay up or go down, and because many clubs are scraping together the cash for transfer fees, vacillating between various offers, and the transfer of one player often sparks other transfers in a chain reaction, June, the time of last-minute panic, is the most hectic time in the transfer market. The fact that most of the people involved are on holiday at that time of year only raises stress levels: agents can't get through to their players because there's no reception for their mobile phones in Mauritius; club directors have difficulty making contact with their managers. Manchester United's Alex Ferguson, for example, had to wait 'till my wife went shopping before I could get to my mobile phone. We were on holiday, after all.'

Alemannia Aachen, who had just been promoted to the Zweite Bundesliga, were considering taking on another goalkeeper, Woodcock had told Lars before the holidays. And now his agent wasn't calling. Perhaps Woodcock had lost the number of the holiday camp Lars and his family were staying in? Perhaps the receptionist had forgotten to pass on Woodcock's message? Lars called him.

'I haven't much time now,' said Woodcock.

'I just wanted to ask you quickly whether anything was happening,' Lars replied.

He didn't only mean that he hadn't much time just at that moment, Woodcock said, he meant that he hadn't much time in general. He was now working for WIGE Media AG, a Cologne agency that marketed football players and football matches. (This was before Woodcock joined Eintracht Frankfurt.) He was sorry, but he couldn't look after Lars any more.

I'd been on the floor for a long time, and now I was getting a kick in the stomach – that was what it felt like when Tony told me – out of the blue – that he had no more time for me. Up until our last phone call he'd only ever said, 'No problem, we'll find a club, no problem.' Now I had a problem, no doubt about it! I got the feeling that Tony hadn't really wanted, hadn't actually dared, to say that to me. If

only he'd told me at least two months before. Now there I was all of a sudden with no club and no agent, and I hardly had any time left. In two weeks most teams would be starting their preparations for the season.

Lars tried to go on with his holiday as though nothing had happened. It was a brilliant holiday – for the children. One day the Leeses visited a tropical garden, but as he talked to his daughter about palm trees and monkeys, Lars reflected on what he could do. He didn't see many possibilities. He had only been a professional footballer for three years; two of those had been abroad, and he had no contacts. In the evening, when Vivian and Christopher were in bed, he called Dirk Heinen and Jens Nowotny, the Leverkusen players with whom he'd stayed vaguely in touch. Heinen said he was always getting calls from agents who wanted to force their services on him. He would mention Lars, he promised.

Just a few days later, Ahmed Bulut was on the phone wanting to speak to Lars Leese.

'I've heard you're looking for a club.'

'Um, yeah.' Lars didn't know who he was talking to.

'I'm an agent. You played in the Premier League, I hear?'

'Um, yeah.'

'Then I've got just the place for you. I have excellent contacts in Turkey. Would you be willing to go there?'

Of course he would have to talk to his wife, but, yes, he would be willing.

'Kocaelispor are looking for a keeper. They were fifth in Turkey last season, and they want to build up a great team. You'd be making three quarters of a million marks [about £250,000].'

He'd certainly give it a thought, said Lars.

'I'll sort it out, and then I'll get back to you, OK?'

Bulut actually did ring back. Meanwhile, Lars talked to Daniela about it. They'd looked in an atlas to see where Kocaeli was – not far from Istanbul, in the western, affluent part of Turkey. Daniela and he were prepared to go anywhere at all, as long as it was soon. But when Bulut rang back he had stopped talking about Turkey.

'Uerdingen KFC want you,' he announced triumphantly.

That meant the German Regionalliga, but Lars wasn't in a position to be choosy. He looked on the bright side: Uerdingen was still a name in football. They'd won the DFB Cup (the equivalent of the FA Cup) in 1985. They'd slipped since then, admittedly, but their aims and their income were still high, and the club's infrastructure was professional.

'They'd pay you 12,000 marks [about £4,000] a month, plus a 1,250 bonus per win,' Bulut added. 'You'd be their leading player.'

That sounded very promising, Lars said.

'Then let's meet on Friday morning at nine thirty in Uerdingen's offices in Krefeld, OK?'

On the Löschenhofweg in Krefeld at half past nine on a Friday in June, Lars had his first meeting with the man who had so quickly got him back into the business. Bulut was born in Donaueschingen, lived in Istanbul, was married to a Swiss woman and was equally at home in all cultures. Lars didn't consider it unusual for an agent simply to phone up and conjure a club out of his hat. On the contrary, he had imagined that that was how things worked in professional football.

Hans-Peter Jakob, the general manager of Uerdingen KFC, was a perfectly friendly man. He confirmed that they would be happy to take on Lars and that they could pay him 12,000 marks a month. 'We have a young goalkeeper here, Christian Vander,' he said. 'He's 19, really first-rate, he's going to be great. But we also need an experienced keeper as a failsafe, someone who's prepared to sit on the subs' bench.' Jakob smiled.

'Excuse me?' said Lars, flabbergasted. 'I was told you were looking for a leading player. Now you're saying I've got to sit on the subs' bench behind a 19-year-old?'

Bulut shifted nervously back and forth on his chair.

Jakob continued to smile. 'We *are* looking for a kind of leading player. A goalkeeper with authority and experience he can pass on to Vander.'

'Sorry, but I like football too much for that. I want to play. I don't want to sit on the subs' bench in the Regionalliga.'

'One moment. Before we talk any further, let's go outside together for a second,' said Bulut, a forced smile on his face, taking Lars by the arm.

When they were standing in the corridor and Jakob's office door had closed, the tone changed.

'Tell me, what kind of an exhibition was that?' Bulut enquired.

'You were talking about a leading player. And now they're saying they mean a leading player on the subs' bench. Are you taking the piss? I've plenty of time to do that when I'm 35. I'm 29, Ahmed.'

'Hey, don't be stupid. You smile and say yes, you sign the contract, **and** then you'll see: the coach will notice that you're the **better** keeper, and then you'll play.'

'I **won't** get that chance. Didn't you hear what he said? They **think** Vander is *the* talented German goalkeeper, and they **want** to build him up. He's sure to be number one, whatever happens. This is all a complete waste of time.'

A minute later they were back in the manager's office, smiling again. Lars told Jakob he was sorry, the job wasn't for him. Jakob thanked him for his frankness. Bulut said nothing and looked insulted. Agents only make money if they pull off the deal.

If Bulut had let him know beforehand that Uerdingen were only really looking for a substitute keeper, Lars would have had a chance to think about whether he should accept the job and try to get Vander out of the way. But in Jakob's office the truth had come so unexpectedly that he hadn't been able to hide his horror. He couldn't smile and say, 'Fine, put me on the bench,' while thinking, 'I'm going to finish Vander off.' He was too taken aback to be insincere.

It would only have been the Regionalliga anyway, he consoled himself on the way back to his holiday camp. And hadn't Bulut been in negotiation with Kocaelispor anyway? 'I haven't heard anything from them yet,' Bulut had told him when they met in Krefeld.

Two weeks later it was July, and in the football world summer holidays had given way to preparations for the coming season. Bulut had another club for him: SV Wilhelmshaven. Regionalliga again. Still no mention of Kocaelispor. Lars went to the North Sea coast for a three-day trial.

'Have you got a family?' coach Hubert Hüring asked him when it was over.

'Yes, a wife and two children.'

'Then you'll need at least 10,000 marks [£3,500] a month, won't you?'

'That's what I've been thinking, yes.'

'We can't pay you that, beanpole. Sorry, but our budget's completely exhausted. I might have been able to get five or six thousand together one way or another, but 10,000 is impossible.'

It was the truth, but at that moment it also happened to suit the club. Hüring wasn't in any great rush to hire Lars. Over the three-day trial he hadn't played all that well. He informed Daniela that he was coming home. After their holiday they had rented a house just outside Frankfurt, in Gelnhausen-Hailer, near to where Daniela's family lived.

Daniela tried to cheer Lars up, but that seldom works when you're unhappy yourself. The endless insecurity, the permanent sense of powerlessness was increasingly getting to her. 'You get up in the morning and you hope something's going to happen,' she reflected. 'You hope someone's going to phone. You go to bed in the evening and think, "Would we go to Turkey?" You ignore the fact that the offer from Turkey is still far from concrete. You clutch at straws. Lars went to Krefeld and I was already looking forward to it. Would we be able to live in Cologne again? Lars went to Wilhelmshaven and I was already thinking, "What would it be like to live by the North Sea?" And then everything collapsed again. All over again, every day. Even China was mentioned once. So you sit there and you think really hard about how you would cope with the language in China. And then you never hear another word from the people who were going to take you to China.'

When she says that, I nod and try not to show any emotion. China was my fault, I fear. Or rather Malaysia. I'd read somewhere that the late ex-Arsenal player David Rocastle had ended his professional career with a Malaysian club and I'd asked Lars why he didn't try to get a job there; in South-East Asia they held anyone who had once played in the English Premier League in incredibly high esteem. 'You think I could get a job there?' he'd asked, and I could already tell from his voice that he was imagining life as a footballing hero in Malaysia. At the time I had no idea how painful it was for him and his wife when such bubbles burst, one after the other.

Whenever I phoned Lars during that time, he struck me as being in good spirits – not euphoric, but as much on top of things as he had ever been. Perhaps I didn't know him well enough. But even Holger Wacker, his good friend from school, didn't think Lars had 'had it' with football. Lars' cheerful personality meant he was always able to put a brave face on things. But the fact that he kept his optimistic smile didn't mean that he was naive enough to hang on to his hopes and dreams at the end of July 1999. He signed on the dole.

At the social security office in Gelnhausen they gave him a form to fill in. As a footballer, he fell into the category 'artistic and other activities'. His alternative careers, he was told, included ventriloquist, clown and flag-waver.

I didn't like going to the social security. You know how people talk: a professional footballer – he's earning millions, and now he's claiming unemployment benefit as well! No one accused me of that, but that was what I automatically thought; that was how I could hear people talking about me in my mind. Then, when the unemployment benefit was brought in line with my income as a footballer and I was getting the maximum available, 3,300 marks (just over £1,000) a month after tax and insurance, I had real difficulties coming to terms with that. I had to justify it to myself: you've never earned millions, Lars, you're only getting that much because you've paid so much in. You're not a leech, you want to work. But I still had a bad feeling. I was getting more for doing nothing than I had earned as a salesman

in a 40-hour week. You feel ashamed, although you know there's no reason to be ashamed.

When the Leeses had taken the house in Hailer at the beginning of July, they'd told the owner, 'We might well move out any second.' Now, five weeks later, they were beginning to get used to their temporary life. The football season had started, and they could no longer act as if they were going to move off the next day. There were always chance events – an injured keeper here, a keeper below form there – but it was more realistic to believe that Lars would find a club by December, when football took its winter break and the transfer market got going again.

Daniela went out to work again for the first time in four years, half-days in a Gelnhausen trading company that bought company cars and sold them on to private individuals. Lars became a house husband. He washed the dishes, did the shopping, played with Christopher, collected Vivian from nursery school, hoovered the house. And when he looked out of the window, he often started to get angry. It had always been important for him to provide for his family. That was no longer his role. Nice as it was to spend so much time with his children, it didn't change the fact that Lars felt as though he'd been relegated. Twelve months earlier he had been the number one keeper at Barnsley Football Club; 22 months ago he had been a hero at Anfield. Now he was standing in a provincial kitchen washing the dishes. He had risen from nowhere into the dream-world of professional football, and been slung back out of it just as violently. He had no defences against the whims of the business. Sometimes, when there seemed no way out and it dragged him down, he watched the Liverpool match on video. His brilliant saves against Riedle, Berger, Leonhardsen, internationals all, always lifted

208

his spirits; but there was always the question: how could he have been forgotten in two years? How could it be that even ambitious Regionalliga clubs weren't queuing to snap him up?

I had my first real taste of Lars' despair on 21 September 1999 in a soft and uncomfortable Glasgow hotel bed. I was in Scotland reporting on the first-round Champions League match between Glasgow Rangers and Bayern Munich for a German newspaper. I'd got back to my hotel very late after a night on the town with some journalist friends, and at ten o'clock in the morning I was still in that troubled state in which you can't lie still and you can't move. Suddenly my mobile rang. It was Lars.

Did I know a good agent? Since his trial in Wilhelmshaven in July he hadn't had a single offer or enquiry. Bulut had said he would keep on looking, and perhaps he was, but Lars didn't really know him – at any rate, he hadn't heard a word from him for weeks. 'Without contacts you're nothing in this business,' said Lars, 'and I have none. I feel so powerless.'

I promised to look into it.

Among the German agents I had met as a football journalist, Heinz Gruler had always made the best impression on me. Gruler, who looked after professional players such as Jean-Marie Pfaff, Oliver Bierhoff and Dietmar Hamann, had been in the business for more than 25 years and still had a very good reputation, which was rare. I had already passed on one player to Gruler, Andre Gumprecht, a likeable boy who had curiously ended up with Lecce in Serie A and was stranded there after a far from glorious year. Gruler had got him a trial with St Gallen FC within a week.

'Oh, sorry,' said Gruler when I called him after I got back

from Glasgow, 'I don't take goalkeepers any more. No point.'

I was dumbfounded. You often heard about players who couldn't find a club, but here we seemed to have a player who couldn't even find an agent.

That had less to do with Lars Leese than with his position. Goalkeepers are particularly hard to agent – inevitably, because every professional club employs a dozen midfield players but only two, or at the most three, goalkeepers. And in no other position is there so little fluctuation. Goalkeepers need security; they aren't moved around as often as other players. For those goalkeepers who don't establish themselves in a safe number one position, there's just 'a small, murderous market', said Gruler's business partner Dirk Lips. For that reason they had sworn to themselves, 'Hands off goalkeepers unless they're absolutely world class or really talented up-and-coming players.'

Half a dozen other German goalkeepers were unemployed at the same time as Lars, and they had all played in the Bundesliga. They included such former stars as Marc Ziegler, who was number one with VfB Stuttgart at the age of 19, and five years later, after being thrown out of Bursaspor in Turkey, was already going through his second period of unemployment. 'Why is he being thrown on the scrapheap at the age of 24?' Ziegler's agent Jürgen Schwab asked furiously. 'At the age of 19, there he was being praised to the skies – super-Ziegler in the national squad, and so on.' Then came a few errors and a new coach. 'All of a sudden you're right down at the bottom of the losers drawer,' said Schwab. Lars was in an even worse position. He was pretty much unknown in Germany, and in England he had most recently been substitute goalkeeper for a First Division club.

I rang Wolfgang Vöge. I still blush at the thought that I was naive enough to imagine a high-profile agent like Vöge, who in the main looked after internationals, would seriously consider representing an unknown 30-year-old goalkeeper. Vöge sighed; fine, get Lars to give me a call. Lars rang him two or three times. During their first conversation Vöge asked what money he hoped to make; subsequently he made it fairly clear to Lars that he wouldn't be wasting his time with a 30-year-old keeper.

But in the Zurich agent Marcel Schmid I finally found someone who was both serious and willing to ask around on Lars' behalf. When people in the business talked about Schmid, they usually said he wasn't 'a typical agent'. That should be seen as a compliment. He had spent 13 years as a journalist, most recently as a presenter on German-speaking Swiss television. Now he was earning most of his money organising and marketing events like the 'Football Arena', an annual symposium. Unlike some agents who are inspired by the desire for money more than anything else, Schmid hadn't forgotten that he wasn't trading in pork-bellies. 'He's the one,' Lars told his wife the first time he spoke to Schmid, 'who's going to get me a job.' Because Schmid was the first one who told Lars, 'Don't get your hopes up.' Hearing that, strange as it may sound, did Lars a lot of good.

I'd had enough of those hot-air merchants who promised the earth, didn't keep their promises and then simply dropped you. There were people who would phone you up out of the blue; you can barely make out their name, but they're from FSV Mainz 05 or wherever. Is it true that I'm still looking for a club and would be available on a free transfer? So I say, yeah, that's right. Great, they're interested. They'll discuss it with the trainer and call again tomorrow. When the phone rang the next day I'd immediately

jump for it, and when it was just a friend calling as usual I'd say, 'Look, we're going to have to keep this short. Mainz 05 are going to call, and they might have something for me.' And the man from the previous day, whoever he might have been, would never call again. I couldn't understand that: someone taking the trouble to get hold of my number and call me up, hear what he wants to hear, and then nothing more. Don't these people know what effect they're having on you? Then your wife and friends ask you in the evening, 'So, do Mainz want you?' And you've got to tell them ten times, 'They never rang back.' The silence after that was always terrible – when your friends have nothing to say. Marcel Schmid was the first one I was sure wouldn't give me any false hopes; he was too honest and realistic to put me through such emotional chaos. Of course that didn't mean that he would get me a club. But I just thought: if it isn't a serious man like him, who's it going to be?

Schmid changed nothing about Lars' everyday life. Now that he was unemployed he was doing a lot of training to keep himself fit. Every day, when Daniela came home from work and took the children off his hands, he went to the gym for two hours. In the evening he trained with the Oberliga club Bernbach SV, and if Bernbach weren't training he played in the next village with the Kreisliga side Melitia Roth. As a midfielder. Both Bernbach and Roth asked him if he'd consider playing for them until he found a professional club.

'You can't do that,' Schmid told him. If he did, Lars would have to register officially as a player with one of the clubs, 'and then what am I supposed to tell professional clubs? At the moment he's playing midfield in the Kreisliga?'

But by now Lars was almost past caring. He just wanted to play football again. It was hard for him to stay cool and not succumb to the blandishments of the amateur clubs.

Once he drove to the Riederwald in Frankfurt to watch Eintracht training, and to see Jan Aage Fjörtoft, his former colleague from Barnsley. When Sven Schmitt, the substitute goalkeeper, had to leave training after an hour due to an injury, Lars scented an opportunity.

'Ask whether you need another goalkeeper for the session this afternoon,' he said to Fjörtoft. Lars always had his goal-keeping kit in the boot of his car. He was on permanent standby.

He wasn't allowed to play, 'for insurance reasons', René Müller, Eintracht's goalkeeping coach, told him. It looked like Lars' luck had deserted him completely.

Meanwhile, Marcel Schmid was mentioning Lars' name here and there. The result was as expected: very few coaches were looking for a goalkeeper, and even fewer had heard of Lars Leese. No one was really showing any interest. 'Lars was neither a young talent nor an experienced, high-profile keeper,' said Schmid. 'That doesn't exactly make clubs prick up their ears.'

The first time they spoke, Schmid had assured Lars that if he heard about an injured goalkeeper he would let him know; he would bear him in mind 'every time I have a meeting with a club. But I'm not going to contact half of Europe on your behalf. Somewhere the relationship between expense and income must be the right one for me as an agent. You can't put as much time into working for a goal-keeper who is, to put it bluntly, on the scrapheap as you can on a 24-year-old international.'

Lars' reaction to this hard truth led Schmid to do more for him than he really wanted to. 'Lars was extraordinarily nice and understanding. When he called he apologised – and this in a business in which 19-year-old Zweite Bundesliga players put pressure on you because you still haven't got them a contract with Inter Milan. The fact that he was such a terrific bloke inspired me to do something for him, but first we had to find a club that would say, "We're taking him because he's such a great guy."'

The winter break came, the transfer market grew frantic again, and Lars was still on the sidelines. He accepted it in silence. He just felt tired.

12

UNCLE RAINER INTERVENES

THAT WINTER, DANIELA could no longer go out to work. She couldn't even walk. Blood actually started to burst out of her feet. She only had to open her hands and the reddened skin would split as though it was made of parchment. She could hardly even dress herself, let alone touch the children or Lars. In the skin clinic in Michelbach near Aschaffenburg her doctor asked her if he could take photographs of her hands and feet. Such advanced psoriasis was a medical phenomenon. Along with his diagnosis, the doctor speculated on the cause, but Daniela had already worked that out: stress. Life in this state of uncertainty had made her ill.

Her husband's fate had always affected her more than it had Lars. When John Hendrie had exiled him to the reserves at Barnsley, she was still suffering on Lars' behalf long after he himself had come to terms with the humiliation. The sudden descent into unemployment had been too much for her nerves. When she came home from her job in Gelnhausen at lunchtime, and Lars sadly told her how trapped he felt standing at the kitchen sink and watching life drifting past, she felt terrible. How could she go to work and feel happy about it?

The tense atmosphere couldn't even be hidden from a four-year-old child. 'My mum's got a husband already,' Vivian would interrupt when she saw her mother in conversation with a man. 'Do you still love Mum?' she constantly asked her father. Losing her friends in Barnsley had been bad enough; now she worried that she was going to lose her family as well – she was too young to understand why her parents were suddenly so unhappy and irritable. 'What's up, Dad, don't you want to play football any more?' she asked.

Christopher, who was two, no longer accepted his mother. Now that Lars was at home all day, he was the one the kids looked to first. Christopher wouldn't leave his side. That only changed months later, when Daniela went on holiday with the children to recuperate after spending six weeks in the skin clinic.

There, Daniela's skin became stronger, but on their own the drugs couldn't effect a complete cure. For that to happen she needed peace and order in her life again. It was around then that Lars stopped hankering after a job in professional football. Now he just wanted things to get back to normal. He hadn't heard anything from Bulut for ages, and the gaps between his telephone conversations with Marcel Schmid were getting bigger and bigger. Professional footballer? It seemed like another life. Now, at half past five in the morning, he was standing in one of the business parks or building sites around Gelnhausen, selling sandwiches. Daniela's Uncle Rainer had lost one of the drivers for his breakfast delivery service. And after all, as Uncle Rainer said, Lars wasn't exactly busy at the moment. In fact it was nice to be doing something again, even if it was only selling bread rolls at the crack of dawn.

Holger Wacker, Lars' old friend from Cologne, didn't

understand it at all. 'You've got all these agents running around the place for you, and none of them can find you a club – that can't be right. They've had nine months now and they haven't done a thing for you. Why don't you sort it out yourself?' That was what Wacker had always done, sorted things out for himself. That was what had made him such a successful estate agent. But this was football, Lars replied; 'I can't just send out a bunch of CVs.'

He had already tried looking for a job on spec. In August 1999, when he had just moved to Gelnhausen, the Zweite Bundesliga club Offenbach visited the nearby village of Meerholz for a friendly. Lars approached Offenbach's general manager Klaus Gerster, introduced himself and asked if he could drop in for a trial. Gerster didn't so much as look at him as he wandered away.

But still Wacker couldn't see it. 'If you think you can't do it without an agent, then just send me along. Tell me what clubs I should go and see, and I'll do it.'

Back in school, when they had been the only two boys in a class of 17, they had insisted that they would bake the best biscuits for the Christmas parties, and they had done. Ten years later, with the same pioneering spirit, Wacker and Lars set about turning themselves into football agents. Lars had accepted his fate with resignation months before; all of a sudden his enthusiasm came back. 'Lars isn't a person with a lot of get up and go,' Wacker later explained in his office, where visitors are dwarfed by the massive, presidential furniture. 'He needs someone to drag him there. But if you say, "Come on, let's do this," he'll go great guns.'

Perhaps they weren't using the most innovative working method, but then good methods needn't always be complicated. Every Monday and Thursday, Lars combed through *kicker* magazine. If he came across an article portraying a goalkeeper in an unfavourable light, or read that someone was looking for a keeper, he immediately passed it on to Wacker. Thus, in February and March 2000 Waldhof Mannheim, 1860 Munich, Alemannia Aachen, Rot-Weiss Essen, Kickers Stuttgart, Fortuna Cologne and FC St Pauli all received faxes from Holger Wacker, referring only to the fact that goalkeeper Lars Leese could be had without a transfer fee, and attaching a copy of Lars' CV. Wacker wrote the faxes on personal notepaper as his company letterhead might not have struck precisely the right note. Wacker Estate Agents represents goalkeeper Lars Leese. Serious bidders only.

If Wacker heard nothing from the clubs, and generally he didn't, he phoned them up. At the office in Aachen they wouldn't put him through to coach Eugen Hach. Mannheim, Stuttgart, St Pauli and Cologne politely declined. Only Rot-Weiss Essen of the Regionalliga called him back.

'Yes, Berge speaking, Rot-Weiss Essen.'

Wacker happened to be in the car with Lars when the call came through.

He had received the fax about Lars Leese, said Berge, and wanted to know what the deal was.

'Yes? Just a moment,' said Wacker, and hissed at Lars: 'Berger or somebody, from Essen. D'you know him?'

Lars shrugged his shoulders.

'Who did you say you were?' asked Wacker.

'I'm sorry? This is Klaus Berge speaking, the coach of Rot-Weiss Essen.'

'Oh, right.'

It was clear to Wacker that the coach hadn't much cared for his question. Wacker apologised; he was just a friend doing Lars Leese a favour, and he didn't want any kind of agent's fee, in fact he didn't know anything about football, so he hadn't known straight away . . .

'Right, listen to me. If you're going to start sending faxes all over the shop, you should at least know who you're sending them to.'

Berge was still a bit offended that they didn't know who he was, but after Wacker had apologised a few more times and explained everything all over again, Berge was able to see the funny side. He really was looking for a goalkeeper. Lars should drop by for a trial some time soon. In fact, it would be better for him to arrange a date with Lars in person over the next few days.

'Fine agent you are! You don't even know the coach's name!' yelled Lars.

'And you're a big help, letting me walk right into that,' Wacker shouted back.

They laughed with relief, almost hysterically. In just a few weeks, they'd achieved more than all the professional agents put together.

Playing agents was starting to be fun. Wacker phoned Helmuth Reuscher, the scout of Bundesliga team 1860 Munich. 1860 had been looking for a goalkeeper for the coming season, Reuscher confirmed, but they'd found one in the form of Karlsruhe's Simon Jentzsch. Wacker just went on talking. Couldn't they meet anyway? Even if 1860 weren't interested, Reuscher might be able to recommend Lars to someone else, or at least give him a few tips about which clubs were still worth looking at. 'I knew the effect Lars had on people,' said Wacker, so I knew that if Reuscher got to meet Lars, he'd try to help us.' He would soon be at the youth tournament in Duisburg-Wedau, said Reuscher, not sounding particularly convinced. Did they want to drop by there?

Lars had played in the same tournament when he was 15. His Mittelrhein team had been up against other regional associations such as Bavaria, Hesse and Lower Saxony. In those days they'd been watched by their parents and dogs; when he went to Wedau with his friend Wacker, dozens of club scouts, youth coaches from Bundesliga teams, agents, insurance representatives and journalists stood on the side-lines. It showed how much the sport had changed in just a decade. Now 15- and 16-year-olds were being wooed so extravagantly that they could believe they were stars even before they were anywhere near a professional squad. Those were the years when gold fever hit the football scene.

Reuscher was the right man to help Wacker and Lars make contacts in the business. As 1860's only full-time scout he watched two or three matches every week, from the Bundesliga to the Oberliga, from Belgium to Bulgaria. He knew the world and his wife, and took a childlike pride in being close to the great men, and the supposedly great men, of the sport. 'I like players to dress nicely, in a suit and so on,' he once told me. 'I like them to be turned out nicely.' Lars, blond, tall and strong, charming and likeable, had the desired effect. Of course he would help him, said Reuscher.

He recommended that Lars get in touch with Mannheim agent Dieter Heimen. In one important respect, Heimen was unlike anyone else who had given Lars advice until then: he had been a goalkeeper himself. In Lars, Heimen didn't just see another hopeless case, he saw himself. Back in 1988, when Schalke 04 hadn't extended his contract, Heimen too had been unemployed for a season. Although he hadn't yet met Lars in person, he managed to arrange a trial with Zweite Bundesliga side Waldhof Mannheim. Three weeks earlier the club had turned the keeper down in response to Wacker's fax. One call from Heimen, and nothing was a problem. It was no small risk for the agent. His reputation could be easily damaged if Lars proved to be a disappointment, but natural solidarity between goalkeepers took precedence.

One Wednesday in April 2000, 11 months after he had last trained with professionals, Lars travelled to Mannheim. When he arrived at ten o'clock, the team wasn't there. 'That's the way it is here,' goalkeeping coach Walter Pradt explained. 'This morning I'll try you out myself. If you're any good, you can train with the team in the afternoon.' An hour and a half later, Pradt told Lars he'd survived the first round. At three o'clock it was time for the real thing.

Late that afternoon, Udo Schöpfer, a reporter on the local daily newspaper *Die Rheinpfalz*, rang me. I'd often written articles from England about a certain German goalkeeper, he said; could I give him any extra information? Mannheim was looking for a new number one, and 'it's probably going to be Leese', Schöpfer added.

At Mannheim I trained ferociously. It wasn't the thought that this could be my last chance that drove me on. It was more the fear of making a fool of myself. The fear of making mistakes made me concentrate incredibly hard, 'You remind me of Ruud Hesp!' Dieter Heimen told me when he saw me for the first time. I've never really considered Ruud Hesp to be a truly great goalkeeper, but at that time he was playing for Barcelona, so Heimen must have meant that as a compliment. In the end I was able to do the rest of the training week. At lunchtimes I went and ate with six or seven of the players, and completely forgot that I was here for a trial. It was as though I was already part of the team. I felt almost too good.

A week later, Heimen called Lars. Waldhof had taken on Achim Hollerieth from VfB Stuttgart as their new goalkeeper.

To be fair, Hollerieth had always been Waldhof's main target, but in April it had looked unlikely that they'd get him. SV Waldhof were strapped for cash and wanted to take the goalkeeper on loan, but Stuttgart had insisted on a transfer fee of 250,000 marks (about £80,000). So Waldhof's coach Uwe Rapolder had started looking around for alternatives. Lars had made a reasonably good impression during training, but, paradoxically enough, that had been to Hollerieth's advantage. When Stuttgart recognised that Waldhof was seriously looking for another goalkeeper, they quickly agreed to let Hollerieth go after all, in return for an 80,000-mark (£25,000) loan fee.

At least, thanks to Dieter Heimen, Lars had managed to get back on to the transfer carousel. After Hollerieth's transfer, VfB Stuttgart was looking for a new substitute goalkeeper. On 26 April, coach Ralf Rangnick tried out three goalkeepers at once: Cesar Thier from Regionalliga club Borussia Fulda, Austrian youth international Hans-Peter Berger, and Lars Leese. Then Rot-Weiss Essen's Klaus Berge invited Lars to a trial on the same day.

Nothing at all for a year, then two requests at exactly the same time.

'Realistically speaking you've more chance of ending up in Essen with a Regionalliga club than with a leading Bundesliga club like Stuttgart,' Wacker told Lars. 'You've always got to go to the biggest club first,' Heimen added. 'You have a go in Stuttgart, and if you can't manage that, then we can still go down and look in the Regionalliga.'

Lars phoned Berge. He was pleased that he got the answering-machine. He turned Berge down.

And then Stuttgart didn't take on any of the three keepers they had tried out.

The fear that had galvanised Lars in Waldhof made him

seize up in Stuttgart. He let in shot after shot, and he knew immediately he'd blown it. 'If you wanted the job,' he thought to himself, 'you should have been able to save balls like that.'

He didn't hear another word from Essen either. Klaus Berge had had enough of him, and one way or another that was quite understandable: first he'd had a friend of Lars' asking who on earth he was, then he'd arranged a trial and Lars had declined to attend. Heimen kept his word and found two Regionalliga clubs, Wacker Burghausen and Carl-Zciss Jena. Lars could earn up to 8,000 marks (about £2,500) a month there.

Precisely a year – a whole football season – had now passed since Lars had left Barnsley.

I didn't need all that any more. It had been nice to be part of things again in Mannheim and Stuttgart, even if it was just for a few days, but that year had worn me down. I'd lost my edge; I didn't want to get back into professional sport at any price. The madness was gone. Danny wasn't having the best of times in Gelnhausen, and Vivian was still suffering from loss anxieties. She kept asking me, 'Dad, we aren't really moving again, are we?' Why should I go to Jena or Burghausen for two or perhaps three years, somewhere in the provinces with which we had absolutely no connection? Just to play for some middling Regionalliga club? I just wanted to put down roots and find peace.

He went to see Winfried Pütz, the chairman of his old club Preussen Cologne. Pütz invited Lars to play for them again in the Oberliga in the coming season. He would also help him to find a job. In fact, Volker Struth, a business partner of Pütz's, was looking for someone to work in his office supplies distribution business.

'Are you really going to pack it in now, just when you're getting back into the transfer market?' Wacker asked him.

'Playing in the Oberliga and holding down an office job? I can find something better for you than that,' said Heimen.

But Lars had had enough of waiting.

At the end of May the Leeses moved back to Hürth. They were back where they'd started. Daniela's hands we're still scarred, but four weeks after returning to the suburbs of Cologne her psoriasis disappeared. In the new flat Vivian asked anxiously a few times, 'We're staying here now, aren't we?' It was nice for Lars to be able to say, at last, 'Yes, we're staying here now.'

Or were they?

'Hey, Softy, listen to this. I've been talking to Eduard, and Cottbus might want you.'

The unmistakeable voice of Uncle Rainer, the breakfast deliveries king from Gründau-Lieblos. But who was Eduard, and what was that about Cottbus?

'Yeah, yeah, that's how it happened,' Uncle Rainer told me later. 'I'm not a shy kind of guy,' he added, and after speaking to him for two minutes I was in no doubt about that.

Uncle Rainer had read in the newspaper *Bild am Sonntag* that Energie Cottbus, recently promoted to the Bundesliga, were looking for a goalkeeper. 'So I think to myself, that can't be true! That great softy Lars has been running around the place for a year and finding nothing, and Cottbus is looking for someone and clearly hasn't a notion Lars exists.' Uncle Rainer told them.

He rang Energie's office. He wanted to speak to Eduard,

he said confidently. (The 'Eduard' in question was Eduard Geyer, Cottbus's coach. Uncle Rainer didn't know him from Adam; more to the point, Geyer didn't even know Rainer existed.) Geyer was with the team on the training ground. Sorry, said the secretary. Then she would have to give him Eduard's mobile phone number, said Uncle Rainer. 'I just want to help you. I have a goalkeeper in the family. He's played in Leverkusen and in England. He'd be just right for you. I'm not an agent or anything, I'm just his uncle.'

'I just turned on the charm with the lady,' explained Uncle Rainer, 'and finally she gave me his mobile number.'

He called Geyer that evening.

'Eduard, it's Rainer here.'

'Listen, I've no time at the moment, I'm just watching a friendly. Call me tomorrow morning.'

Geyer was thinking to himself: Rainer? Who the hell is Rainer?

He asked the question when Uncle Rainer rang him back.

'I'm just Rainer, and apart from that I'm nobody. I have a breakfast delivery service here in Gründau-Lieblos, but that's not what I'm calling about. I'm calling about a goalkeeper.'

When Uncle Rainer had explained everything, Geyer started laughing. He'd never heard anything like it before. He knew the goalkeeping coach at Leverkusen and would find out about Lars Leese from him. Geyer had played with Werner Friese in Dresden in the fifties.

Two days later, Geyer rang the breakfast delivery service in Lieblos. 'Boss, Eduard Geyer's on the phone,' one of his employees called out. Uncle Rainer still enjoys that moment. 'Imagine: I'm out in the courtyard, and she's shouting, "Eduard Geyer on the phone for the boss!"'

He had arranged with Friese for Lars to drop in at a training session at Leverkusen on Saturday, Geyer told Uncle

Rainer. Friese would then tell him how fit Lars was, and they'd take it from there.

'Have you got time to go there on Saturday, Softy?' Uncle Rainer asked Lars.

It was Saturday 12 August, the first day of play in the 2000/01 Bundesliga season. The Oberliga hadn't started yet. In Leverkusen, the players who hadn't been selected for the match against Wolfsburg – Frank Juric, the third-choice keeper, and other players like Frankie Hejduk, Pascal Ojigwe and Robson Ponte – were training. Lars looked just like one of them, a real professional.

He asked Friese what he would say to Geyer.

'I don't know,' answered Friese. 'You looked good today, but I haven't seen you for two years. I can't really judge.'

Then I said, 'Werner, come on, just recommend me to Geyer. Even if they don't take me, I'm not so bad that I'm going to make a fool of you in a trial here.' But the moment I had heard I was going to see Werner Friese I knew nothing would come of it. Werner's an excellent goalkeeping coach, but he's not the type to stick his neck out. He's always worried about his reputation.

And that was what happened: Friese told Geyer he wasn't sure and Lars was never given a trial at Cottbus. In the end, the only good that came out of it was that Uncle Rainer had made a new friend. He told Geyer they should go for a beer if he ever happened to be in the area.

EPILOGUE:

LARS' DREAM

A T SIX O'CLOCK on Wednesday evenings in Sportpark West, nicknames are all you're likely to hear. Fischi passes the ball to Schuchi, Schuvi's unmarked, Wynni sees the danger and shouts to Embi 'Watch out for Schuvi!', but the ball's already with Klinge. In this world, Lars Leese is still 'Beanpole'.

Klinge is in front of him, it's only seven yards to the goal, and Beanpole bends forwards and seems to contract as though he were a catapult about to be fired. When Klinge shoots, the tension is discharged. Beanpole leaps, out goes the hand, his fingertips outstretched, and he flips the ball around the post and lands on the grass on his chin.

That's the moment when there's no difference between the Premier League and kicking a ball about in the park: the feeling of happiness you get after a brilliant save is always the same. And it's the same for Lars Leese. He's back on his feet straight away – goalkeepers who have let in a goal stay on the ground and goalkeepers who have made a good save jump up immediately and go on playing as though nothing has happened – he rolls the ball to Wynni, Wynni passes it to Kalle, and training with the reserve team of Bundesliga side Borussia Mönchengladbach continues. It's October 2001, and once again football is just a bit of fun as far as Lars Leese is concerned.

Three months earlier we'd been sitting by the Rhine in Cologne and Lars was telling me in a calm, detached voice that his heart wasn't in it any more. After only a year he had resigned from Preussen Cologne, disappointed with his own performance, annoyed that the Oberliga club hadn't paid him the expenses they'd promised him. Fifteen minutes before kick-off at one game in Ratingen, Lars had taken off his gloves and threatened to go home if he didn't see at least part of his money. Lars didn't put his gloves back on until chairman Winfried Pütz himself came on to the pitch and handed him 1,000 marks (over £300) in 100-mark notes. 'My year of unemployment left me completely disillusioned,' he said as we sat by the Rhine, 'and that problem with the money at Preussen was the final straw. I didn't enjoy playing, so I didn't play well. And if I didn't play well, I enjoyed it even less the following week. I'd just had it with football.' He thought that if he was to start enjoying it again he would have to go back to where his career had started, on the ashpit in Neitersen. But little in his career has happened the way he imagined it would, so why should it start doing so now?

A week before the start of the amateur season with Sportfreunde Neitersen, he got a call from Holger Fach. They had played together at Bayer Leverkusen. Today, Fach is the coach of the Mönchengladbach amateurs, as the reserve team is traditionally known, despite the fact that the players have trained and been paid as professionals for a long time now. Fach's goalkeeper had broken his shin, the season was around the corner, and it wasn't easy for him to find someone he trusted to put in goal. Could Lars help him out for six months, or even a year?

In the gloom of Mönchengladbach's Sportpark West, from 30 yards away you can't make out the faces of the players when Schuvi loses the ball to Embi and Schuchi runs into the gap to take the through-pass. None of them is older than 23, which is the point of the reserve team: to train up young players for the Bundesliga squad. And jumping around among them is Lars Leese, 32 years old. He's a guest in the professional game once again, even if he's only on its outskirts. For an hour and a half of training every day he sits in a time machine and experiences at least a hint of the world he lived in for three years in Leverkusen and Barnsley. For an hour and a half he's right back there, even though he's been living in another world for ages now.

In the morning, while the young professionals of Mönchengladbach are busy with their first training session, he is sitting in a business park in the town of Frechen at the premises of Engels & Co., Office Supplies, taking orders. In the afternoon, when his team-mates are having their midday nap or sitting in a café, he is trudging around with the Engels catalogue, *Everything for the Office*, under his arm trying to convince the buyers at various companies that they should order Engels pencils, Engels print cartridges and Engels everything else through him. It isn't easy, especially if ten other reps have already been there with the same purpose in mind. He always has to pull himself together whenever he walks into a new company – not thinking, 'I'm just wasting their time,' but thinking, 'It's your job, Lars.' If he goes in feeling insecure, he usually comes out walking on air. They may not want to place an order, but they're always glad to see him. There aren't many days when he isn't happy to go to work.

In the evening, at half past five, when the Gladbach reserves are changing in the Bökelberg Stadium, he's usually still on the autobahn. He drives straight to Sportpark West. There's a little shed there where they keep balls, nets and other training paraphernalia. There, under a dim light-bulb, he quickly gets changed while his colleagues are being ferried over in Mercedes minibuses marked WE ARE BORUSSIA.

He's still close to professional football — but at the same time he's so very far away.

My time as a professional seems a long way off now. On Monday evenings they show the highlights of the foreign leagues on television, and once when a Liverpool game was on I said to my wife, 'I've played there!' As I said it, I surprised even myself. Lars, you've played in a stadium like that! It struck me as incredible. Christopher always shouts, 'Dad!' and points to the television if there's a sports programme on. Even if it isn't football, even if it's tennis. As far as he's concerned it's clearly quite natural for him to see me on television. But sometimes when I see the old videos from Barnsley, the opposition attacking and the keeper making the save, I'm completely dumbfounded. That's me! It's as though it was another life.

Even during the three years in which he actually was a professional, he had always believed that it wasn't really his life. He always felt like a visitor in the world of professional football. He was more of a fan who had happened to end up on the other side of the fence, and at some point he would wake up and find he was a businessman from Cologne again, going to play after work, just for the fun of it. And that's exactly how things turned out in the end. But were things destined to be that way? To put the question differently: was it just a matter of good luck that Lars Leese had become a professional? Or was it bad luck that his career had lasted for such a short time?

If the Hibernian deal had come off, in all likelihood Lars would still be a professional footballer today. Or if he had found an agent like Dieter Heimen nine months earlier. Or if he'd never eaten that bad chicken. On the other hand, without a lot of luck – and a lot of help – he would never have made it to England. And Dieter Heimen got him another couple of chances with Waldhof Mannheim and VfB Stuttgart. And the dodgy chicken had only knocked him out for a season; it hadn't ended his career in Barnsley.

Perhaps Lars Leese was lucky to have been a professional *and* unlucky that his career had lasted for such a short while.

'He certainly was good enough to be a professional,' says David Watson, Lars' friend and rival in Barnsley's goal. Watson is sitting in the depths of Oakwell on a blue massage table. In the corner is a skeleton, a plastic one. The new, modern training academy has been completed, built with the money from the club's single year in the Premiership; there is now a generous-sized treatment room for injured players. It's the only room Watson still uses here. He never recovered from his knee injury in the summer of 1999. He's an invalid at 26. 'You see,' he says, nodding towards his knee, 'it's tiny things that decide whether or not you can make it in professional football. I twisted my knee, and it was all over. In his second year, Lars unfortunately came up against John Hendrie, who wouldn't let the foreigners play. And that was that as far as Lars was concerned.'

Watson hobbles over to the ice-machine on his crutches, and shovels ice into a cool-box he's brought with him. He needs four shopping-bags of ice a day to cool his knee. I carry the cool-box as we go outside. His father is waiting in the car to drive him home. Among the pictures in the corridor, right by the entrance, there hangs a photograph of Watson in his goalkeeper's kit; his childlike face with its penetrating blue eyes smiles shyly. He was on the way to becoming one of the best in England. 'I was really shocked today when you told me that Lars didn't become a professional until he was 26,' he says, ignoring the photographs. 'He had everything – the moves, the technique, the lot, as though he'd been working professionally for years and years. Can you explain why I bothered training so much when Lars could be as good as he was even without working hard?' Watson laughs.

When he's gone, I go into the empty stadium to say good-bye to Oakwell. It's only three years since Barnsley last played in the Premier League here. I can still hear them shouting, 'We are Premier League, say we are Premier League!' *It feels like another life*, Lars had said. But what a life.

Once, in the year 2000, Barnsley came close to promo-tion again, but they didn't make it and disappeared back to where they had been stuck for decades, in the medi-ocrity of the First Division. 'We all live in hope,' says Ian McMillan, the poet. 'And yet, even if we got back into the Premier League, it wouldn't be the same. It's never the same as it was the first time.' When he told his children, 'I'm going to be talking about Lars Leese,' they had to think for a minute before they answered, 'Oh, yes, Lars Leese.' 'That depressed me,' says McMillan. 'It was our golden year, but people forget so quickly. In a few years' time people will only remember how tall he was. "Oh, yes, the German giant." All that remains of Georgi Hristov is: "Oh, yeah, Georgi, the one who said Barnsley women were ugly." Isn't that sad?'

Many people I spoke to remembered Lars very clearly, I

consoled him. 'Oh, that cheers me up. I'm glad about that,' he said.

At home in Hürth, Lars' son Christopher is already wearing goalkeeper's gloves. Not that he wants to be a goalkeeper. He's four; he wants to score goals. They all do. He only wears his father's gloves at home for running about in. Vivian is in her first year at school, Daniela is learning to be a fitness trainer. The only souvenir of his life as a professional is Lars' phrase 'I've got today off', which he uses whenever there's no training in Mönchengladbach – although of course he still has to work for Engels until five.

There's no place for bitter thoughts in his life.

I see the lads in the reserve team in Mönchengladbach who have been living to play in the Bundesliga since they were 17, and the reality is that only one or maybe two of them will ever get there. I was still playing in goal in the Kreisliga when I was 23, and I made it. I played about 20 professional matches. How could I be bitter about the fact that my professional career came to an abrupt end? I'm happy that I had that career at all. I lived a dream. It was just that I was in professional football for such a short time that it never became real to me. I didn't end up saying, 'Oh Christ, back to Grimsby. They have tiny dressing-rooms and idiot supporters. Do I really have to?' Professional football never became my everyday life. It was only ever a dream. But it was a wonderful dream.

It is growing dark in Sportpark West. There are no floodlights, and the sky is almost as black as the players' tracksuits. In the midst of the 20-year-old boys convinced that they're going to be professionals, Lars Leese is again one of us, a dreamer. Those of us who take Eintracht Frankfurt to victory in the Champions League with a perfect volley into the far corner while we sit on the tube to the office. 'Nice church,' we say to our girlfriends as we stand in front of the cathedral in Milan on holiday, but what we're really thinking about is what it must be like to be cheered off the pitch for Inter when they've just won the championship. Lars Leese is still dreaming as well: if Gladbach's Bundesliga goalkeeper Jörg Stiel gets a three-week suspension, and second goalkeeper Bernd Meier happens to get injured at the same time, and third goalkeeper Uwe Kamps is still five weeks away from match fitness . . .

'I thought I told you to collect the balls, Beanpole!' snaps coach Holger Fach. 'It's going home time!'

But Beanpole is still practising his goal-kicks. They won't get him off the pitch as easily as that.